starting out:
the dutch defence

NEIL MCDONALD

EVERYMAN CHESS

www.everymanchess.com

First published in 2004 by Gloucester Publishers plc (formerly Everyman Publishers plc), Northburgh House, 10 Northburgh Street, London EC1V 0AT

British Library Cataloguing-in-Publication Data
A catalogue record for this book is available from the British Library.

ISBN 978 1 85744 377 6

Distributed in North America by The Globe Pequot Press, P.O Box 480,
246 Goose Lane, Guilford, CT 06437-0480.

All other sales enquiries should be directed to Everyman Chess, Northburgh House, 10 Northburgh Street, London EC1V 0AT
tel: 020 7253 7887 fax: 020 7490 3708
email: info@everymanchess.com; website: www.everymanchess.com

EVERYMAN CHESS SERIES (formerly Cadogan Chess)
Chief advisor: Byron Jacobs
Commissioning editor: John Emms
Assistant editor: Richard Palliser

Typeset and edited by First Rank Publishing, Brighton.
Cover design by Horatio Monteverde.
Printed and bound in the US.

Contents

Bibliography

Books

The Dutch for the Attacking Player, Steffen Pedersen (Batsford 1996)
   This is a repertoire book based on the Leningrad Dutch
Positional Play, Mark Dvoretsky & Artur Yusupov (Batsford 1996)
   This book contains a short but excellent article by Kramnik and Khenkin on the Stonewall
Leningrader System, Stefan Kindermann (Chessgate 2002)
   Published in German language
The Dutch Leningrad, Neil McDonald (Chess Press 1997)
Understanding the Leningrad Dutch, Valery Beim (Gambit 2002)
Dutch Stonewall, Jacob Aagaard (Everyman 2000)
Classical Dutch, Jan Pinski (Everyman 2002)
Play the Classical Dutch, Simon Williams (Gambit 2003)
Dutch Defense: New and Forgotten Ideas, Nikolay Minev & John Donaldson (Thinkers' Press 2003)

Websites and Periodicals

ChessPublishing.com (on running 'Daring Defences' section by Glenn Flear, with contributions by Neil McDonald and Jonathan Tisdall)
Chess Informant
The Week in Chess
ChessBase Magazine

Introduction

Welcome to the often exhilarating, sometimes frustrating, but always exciting world of the Dutch Defence. After 1 d4 the reply 1...f5 causes an immediate imbalance in the position, in the same way that after 1 e4 the most fighting move is 1...c5. In the Dutch, Black is looking for a double-edged game with winning chances right from the onset. It is no wonder therefore that it has attracted the attention of some of the most creative players throughout the history of chess.

It was there right in the beginning, being a favourite of Paul Morphy, the world's best player in the 1850s, who saw it as the quickest way to inject dynamism into the opening struggle. He conceded a draw in a match with Harrwitz in 1858, but won every other serious game with it. True, there were only four top class games, as in those days 1 d4 was regarded as an 'irregular' move!

Other great players who loved the Dutch Defence include Alekhine, Botvinnik, Bronstein and Tartakower. These days, grandmasters Mikhail Gurevich and Vladimir Malaniuk are its chief patrons.

Veselin Topalov and Vladimir Kramnik played the Dutch as young men, but once they reached the highest echelons of chess they both gave it up. I suspect this was because when they were rising stars, playing opponents of a wide assortment of strengths, they were impatient to win all their games as Black. They didn't want to risk a solid opening such as the Slav, in case an unimaginative opponent played for a draw (for example, with the dull Slav Exchange variation). But once they reached the top and were playing exclusively versus other elite players, there was no need to fear that the opponent would kill the game off. Kasparov and Shirov don't play for draws as White!

This brings us to the best feature of the Dutch: there is simply no way for White to deaden the struggle. Whether he likes it or not, he is in for a fight. Bent Larsen made the following comment when faced with a solid but rather passive grandmaster: 'Against such players I like to play the Dutch, as often they potter about too much, so that you can just sit and build up an attack on the kingside.'

If you play the Dutch you have to accept the element of risk. Some years ago I heard a young player moaning to British GM Jonathan Mestel that he had played the risky Sicilian Dragon and been wiped off the board. Mestel, himself a Dragon aficionado, replied calmly 'think of all the draws you have avoided by playing the Dragon.' The same can be said about the Dutch. Personally I have had some truly awful defeats with the Dutch, but these are balanced by wins against Grandmasters which I would never have gained if I had just aimed for a safe game as Black. Playing the Dutch undoubtedly reduces the ratio of draws against weaker opponents and gives chances of unexpected success against stronger opponents.

Which Variation should I play?

It is important to decide which variation of the Dutch most suits your style. I suggest you quickly play through the illustrative games in Chapters 4-8 and then ask yourself: 'in which games did I feel I understood the flow of Black's strategy best?' or conversely 'were there any moves or ideas that seemed completely alien to the way I like to play chess?' You should be able to judge in which chapter you felt most 'at home'.

Of course, it is possible you might hate Black's position in every chapter! In that case you won't be alone: the English grandmaster Matthew Sadler related in a *New in Chess* article that at first he hated Black's position in the Leningrad Dutch because of the hole on e6, but once he learned to live with this defect he began to use the Leningrad himself with success. There is, indeed, a certain 'ugliness' about Black's set-up in the Dutch that can be off-putting: even the first move 1...f5 can make us involuntarily shudder because it seems to go against everything we have learnt about the need to protect the f7-square. Once you have tested the Dutch in some tournament and club games, and hopefully have won some nice games with it, you should start to appreciate its finer qualities.

There are also practical considerations, such as the element of risk involved in each line and the amount of theory that needs to be learnt. As a rule, the more theory attached to a line, the more it is dominated by tactics rather than strategy, and vice versa.

The 'Big Three' Variations in the Dutch

To help you decide what to adopt as your main weapon, here is a quick summary of the three main variations in the Dutch.

The Stonewall Variation

The Stonewall is the most solid, if least adventurous, way of handling the Dutch. It involves putting two pawns on the fourth rank in the centre and denying White the space to launch a direct attack. A typical sequence is 1 d4 f5 2 g3 Nf6 3 Bg2 e6 4 Nf3 d5 5 c4 c6 6 0-0 Bd6 **(Diagram 1)**.

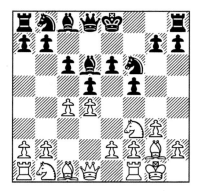

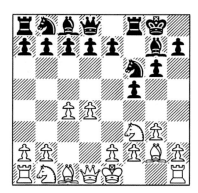

Diagram 1 (W)
The Stonewall

Diagram 2 (W)
The Leningrad Dutch

You should play like this if you like the Queen's Gambit or Slav, as a heavyweight positional battle results. It is the least theoretical and tactical of the big three Dutch variations.

The Leningrad Dutch

This is the sharpest, most counterattacking and riskiest variation of the Dutch. It involves putting the dark-squared bishop on g7, for example 1 d4 f5 2 Nf3 Nf6 3 c4 g6 4 g3 Bg7 5 Bg2 0-0 **(Diagram 2)**.

The bishop is excellently placed there, as it aims at the d4-square and is a tough defender of the black king.

Compared to the Stonewall, Black makes no immediate bid for space in the centre, which means White's pieces have more freedom to make combinations and launch attacks. The pace of the game is therefore faster, and not surprisingly it has accumulated a lot of theory over the years. There will be a lot of other people besides you and your opponent involved in the game! It should appeal to players who like the King's Indian Defence as Black.

The Classical Dutch

This is a halfway house between the Stonewall and Leningrad regarding the amount of theory and element of risk. The usual opening sequence is 1 d4 f5 2 g3 Nf6 3 Bg2 e6 4 Nf3 Be7 5 0-0 0-0 6 c4 d6 **(Diagram 3)**. Black's set-up is marked by its flexibility. He has kept the option of playing in Leningrad or King's Indian style with moves such as ...e6-e5 or ...Bf6 in the future, whilst he is also ready to switch to a central blockade in the style of the Stonewall with ...d6-d5 if appropriate. Of course there is a thin line between flexibility and indecision, and Black has to be careful that he doesn't end up with the worst, rather than the best, features of the other two main lines: namely a centre that is less than secure coupled with little dynamic play. A player experienced in the Nimzo-Indian might be particularly adept at handling Black's mini centre.

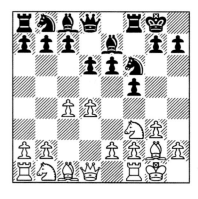

Diagram 3 (W)
The Classical Dutch

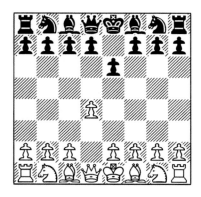

Diagram 4 (W)
Ready for a French?

TIP: Don't ignore the Stonewall!

At first, you might think that there is nothing in common between the Stonewall and the Leningrad or Classical Variations, besides the fact that Black has played 1...f5. However, as your knowledge of the Dutch deepens, you will realise that it is often vital for Black to put a pawn on the d5-square in the early middlegame, even if the game has started with a Leningrad or Classical pawn configuration.

TIP: Even if you intend to make the Leningrad or Classical your weapon of choice, it is essential you know how to handle the Stonewall pawn structure.

What is the best Move Order?

In this book we assume the starting sequence 1 d4 f5, but there can be advantages in other move orders. As will be seen, being able to play the French versus 1 e4 is very useful.

Aiming for a Leningrad

After 1 d4, if Black intends to fianchetto on g7 then really the only alternative to 1...f5 is 1...d6, so that if 2 c4 or 2 Nf3 then 2...f5 followed by 3...Nf6 and 4...g6 etc. is possible. This move order sidesteps the various second move alternatives for White after 1...f5 and is often used by Leningrad Dutch maestro Mikhail Gurevich. But the big question is, should White choose to play 2 e4, are you ready for the Pirc or Modern Defence?

Aiming for a Classical

Here choosing the move order 1 d4 e6 **(Diagram 4)** 2 c4 f5 avoids the Staunton Gambit and 2 Bg5 or 2 Nc3 lines. But this will only be okay if you aren't afraid of the French Defence after 2 e4!.

Aiming for the Stonewall

Here Black has enormous flexibility; the familiar pawn centre could even emerge from a Slav after 1 d4 d5 2 c4 c6 3 Nc3 e6 4 e3 f5. More typically, there is the move order 1...e6 2 Nf3 f5 3 c4 d5, but remember, White can cross your plans with 2 e4 transposing to the French Defence. Most importantly, the Stonewall is often arrived at via the Classical, if Black decides to play ...d6-d5.

I hope you enjoy exploring the variations in this book and emerge with an excellent new weapon against 1 d4. Whichever line of the Dutch you decide to play (perhaps it will be all three!?), I wish you the best of luck in your games!

Neil McDonald,
Gravesend,
December 2004

Chapter One

Dutch Gambit Lines

 **1 d4 f5 2 h3**

 **1 d4 f5 2 g4**

 **The Staunton Gambit**

1 d4 f5 2 h3

I expect you are itching to try out the Dutch in your own games as soon as possible, even before finishing this book. Therefore, rather than demonstrate the elaborate grandmasterly manoeuvres of the Leningrad Dutch, to begin with I have the more modest aim of showing you how to avoid being checkmated in under ten moves. It would be embarrassing if that happened in front of your friends in your first game in the Dutch, right? I mean something like this:

A first round knockout in the Dutch: 1 d4 f5 2 h3

1 d4 f5 (Diagram 1)

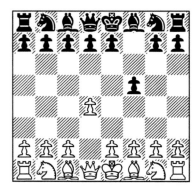
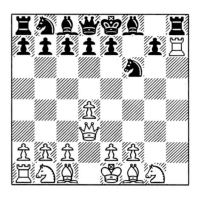

Diagram 1 (W)	**Diagram 2 (B)**
White to play and win?	A Dutch nightmare!

2 h3

A good start to your Dutch career. Your opponent evidently has no idea how to meet it.

2...Nf6 3 g4

...and now White drops a pawn. Things are getting even better!

3...fxg4 4 hxg4 Nxg4 5 Qd3 Nf6

Black is just a pawn up for nothing, right?

6 Rxh7!! 1-0 (Diagram 2)

Wrong: if Black stops mate on g6 he drops the rook on h8. Therefore he has nothing better to do than reset the pieces and try 1...f5 again – if he dares! This has happened countless times, for example in the game Maly-Schmid, Hamburg 1989.

White has exploited the fundamental structural weakness created in Black's kingside by 1...f5 to deliver a sucker punch.

Black strikes back

My advice is don't get involved in White's party tricks: after 2 h3 Nf6
3 g4 proudly decline the pawn on offer with 3...d5! **(Diagram 3)**.

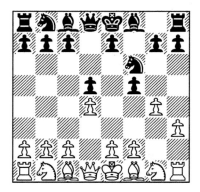

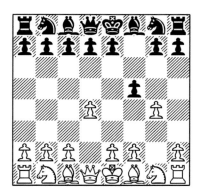

Diagram 3 (W)	**Diagram 4 (B)**
Black plays 3...d5!	Another gambit

This frees the bishop on c8 and strengthens Black's hold on the centre. Now it is White who is looking silly, as why exactly has he played
the moves 2 h3 and 3 g4, which just weaken *his* kingside? A possible
continuation is 4 g5 Ne4 5 Bf4 e6 6 Nf3 c5 7 e3 Qb6 and Black is already calling the shots.

**NOTE: These gambit lines force you to concentrate hard for a few
moves in the opening to avoid disaster, but get it right and the rest
of the game should be less of a challenge than in the other chapters
in this book.**

1 d4 f5 2 g4

A blood brother of 2 h3 is the more direct 2 g4?!.

1 d4 f5 2 g4?! (Diagram 4)

This rivals 2 Kd2 as being the second worst move on the board (I'll
leave you to work out the worst move). Now 2...d5 is possible, but
White is getting more than he deserves in being able to play 3 gxf5
Bxf5, when he has managed to exchange a wing pawn for a centre
pawn without wasting a tempo on 2 h3. So this time we will accept
the pawn with 2...fxg4!. Now 3 h3 aims to open all the lines on the
kingside after 3...gxh3 4 Nxh3!?, when an attack follows on h7 with
Qd3 and Ng5, etc. But Black can cross White's plans with the neat
trick 3...g3!, returning the pawn in order to keep the kingside blocked
and prevent White gaining a lead in development. Then after 4 fxg3
d5 5 Nf3 Nf6 6 Bg2 e6 followed by ...Bd6 etc. Black has a solid centre,

which is more than can be said for White's kingside.

TIP: The antidote to these gambits is ...d7-d5!

Game 1
☐ **M.Callinan** ■ **A.Saidy**
Aspen 1968

1 d4 f5 2 g4

Another rather primitive attack on f5 is possible with 2 Qd3, when a good reply is 2...d5!, after which the f5-pawn is defended and 3 e4 prevented. Black can then adopt a Stonewall set-up (as in Chapter 4) with ...Nf6, ...e7-e6, and maybe even ...b7-b6 and ...Ba6 to take direct advantage of the white queen. The only way to justify the queen on d3 is with 3 g4, but then 3...fxg4 4 h3 g3! 5 fxg3 Nf6 6 Nc3 Nc6!? 7 Bf4 e6 8 0-0-0 Bb4 9 Bg2 0-0 looks safe enough for Black.

NOTE: You aren't required to memorise all the variations given in the illustrative games. It is enough to play through them and grasp the general trends behind the moves.

2...fxg4 3 e4

Having pushed aside the f5-pawn, White gets to create his perfect centre. Alas, for him it only lasts for one move.

3...d5! 4 e5 Bf5 5 Nc3 c5! (Diagram 5)

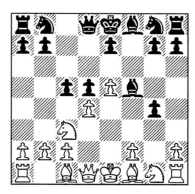
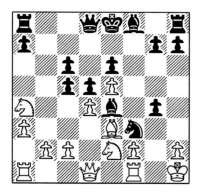

Diagram 5 (W)	Diagram 6 (W)
Nice for Black	A good time to resign

Not only is Black a pawn up, but the extra pawn prevents White developing his knight to f3. Therefore this attack on d4 is all the more effective.

6 Bb5+ Nc6 7 Bxc6+ bxc6 8 Nge2 e6

The position could be compared to that in the Caro-Kann after 1 e4 c6 2 d4 d5 3 e5 Bf5 4 Nc3 e6 5 g4 Bg6 6 Nge2 c5. Naturally it favours Black that the pawn on g4 belongs to him rather than White.

9 Be3 Ne7!

The knight heads all the way to f3 to exploit the weakness in White's kingside.

10 a3?!

White prepares an unfortunate knight manoeuvre that hastens his demise, but his position was already rotten for if 10 dxc5 then 10...Ng6 etc.

10...Ng6 11 Na4? Nh4 12 0-0 Nf3+ 13 Kh1 Be4 (Diagram 6) 0-1

A possible finish is 14 Nac3 Qh4 15 Bf4 Nxh2+ 16 Nxe4 Nf3+ 17 Kg2 Qh3 mate.

We can conclude that White has failed in his first clumsy attempt to prove the Dutch has no right to exist. A much more dangerous challenge awaits Black in the next section.

The Staunton Gambit

This gambit is named after Howard Staunton, the best player in the world in the 1840s. It goes

1 d4 f5 2 e4!? (Diagram 7)

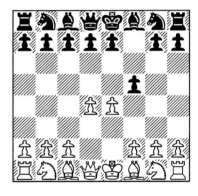

Diagram 7 (B)
The Staunton Gambit

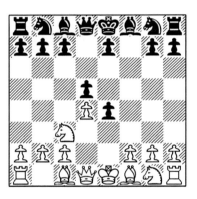

Diagram 8 (W)
3...d5 – not good!

Alas, along with Fischer versus Karpov in 1975, one of the most famous non-matches of all time was that between Staunton and his great rival Paul Morphy in 1858. Therefore, we never got the chance to see what the Dutch devotee Morphy would have done against the Staunton Gambit, as no one else played 2 e4 against the American genius. Perhaps he would have chosen to avoid it, as a couple of times he adopted the move order 1 d4 e6 2 c4 f5.

Theoretical?

Like most gambits with a long history, the Staunton Gambit has accumulated its fair share of theory over the years. Whereas the g2-g4 lines above were naïve to say the least, the Staunton deserves respect as it has been played as White by top grandmasters, including the world-class player Teimour Radjabov. Therefore you definitely need to know the basic theoretical moves.

The Oldest Trick in the Dutch Book

WARNING: If you want to play the Dutch well, you have to keep your eyes open all the time for tactics. You won't get very far relying exclusively on general principles.

After 1 d4 f5 2 e4 fxe4 3 Nc3 it looks like Black can support the pawn with 3...d5? **(Diagram 8)**, but this fails to 4 Qh5+ g6 5 Qxd5 and White regains his pawn whilst leaving the pawn on e4 terminally weak. A variation on the same theme is 3...Nf6 4 Bg5 d5? 5 Bxf6 exf6 6 Qh5+ g6 7 Qxd5 and again Black is in big trouble as after 7...Qxd5 8 Nxd5 he can't defend both c7 and f6.

The Faded Glory of White's 4 f3 Gambit

In the olden days of chess, when defensive technique was far less advanced than today, it is no wonder that 2 e4 enjoyed a great popularity. After 2...fxe4 3 Nc3 Nf6 4 f3 Black would feel honour bound to take on f3, when after 4...exf3? 5 Nxf3 **(Diagram 9)**

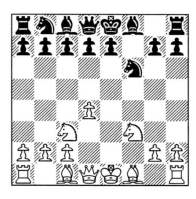

Diagram 9 (B)
Dangerous for Black

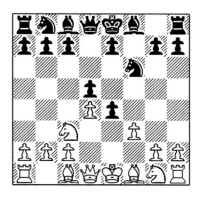

Diagram 10 (W)
Presence in the centre

White has a lead in development, open lines for his pieces and a ready attack. Perhaps a computer could snatch material in this way and then defend stoically and win, but for the rest of us it would be an onerous task.

With 4 f3 White has blocked the best square for his knight on g1 and lost time with his development; so why on earth should Black play 4...exf3, helping him out of his predicament? Therefore, these days Black prefers 4...d5! **(Diagram 10)**.

You might think that after 5 fxe4 dxe4 the pawn on e4 looks ugly, but don't forget that it is an extra centre pawn and performing a valuable strategical function in denying White's knight the f3-square. Play could continue 6 Bg5 Bf5 7 Bc4 Nc6 8 Nge2 e6 and Black is ready to play 9...Qd7 followed by castling queenside. You will notice that he has refused to fall behind in development or hand over open lines to his opponent.

The Positional Approach with 4 Bg5

The plan of f2-f3 has gone out fashion because of the ...d7-d5! response. Instead White has championed the more positional 4 Bg5!?. The basic idea is to play Bxf6 and then Nxe4, when White not only regains his pawn but also has one knight centralised on e4 and the other enabled to go to its natural square on f3 again. Here is an extreme example in which this plan enjoys a remarkable success.

I make no excuses for showing you the following pretty miniature, even though it is hardly going to increase your enthusiasm for the Dutch. To be fair to the loser, it was an off-hand game, so we have no way of knowing the circumstances in which it was played. Sir George Thomas beat both Capablanca and Botvinnik in tournament games, so his king didn't always end up having to make a death march to the other side of the board.

Game 2
☐ **Ed.Lasker** ■ **G.Thomas**
London 1912

1 d4 f5 2 e4 fxe4 3 Nc3 Nf6 4 Bg5 e6?!

An insipid move that makes no effort to fight for space in the centre.

5 Nxe4 Be7 6 Bxf6! Bxf6 7 Nf3

By giving up the bishop pair, White has removed the only black piece that was challenging his excellently placed knight on e4. It is true the knight can be driven away with 7...d5, but this would leave Black with serious structural weakness along the e-file: a backward pawn on e6 and a hole on e5.

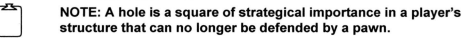

NOTE: A hole is a square of strategical importance in a player's structure that can no longer be defended by a pawn.

7...0-0 8 Bd3

More energetic is 8 Qd2, which keeps in reserve the possibility of developing the bishop on b5, for example if 8...Nc6 9 0-0-0 d5 10 Nxf6+ Qxf6 11 Bb5 when the e5-square is going to fall into the knight's hands after a subsequent Bxc6 and Ne5.

8...b6

Black comes up with the plan of attacking e4 with his queen's bishop: strategically a good idea, but now things happen very quickly on the kingside.

9 Ne5!?

Rather over-optimistic, though it works brilliantly.

9...Bb7?!

Allowing one white knight the freedom of the centre can be put down to carelessness, but two knights is inexcusable. He should have played 9...Bxe5 when 10 dxe5 Nc6 is awkward for White as the e5-pawn is loose.

10 Qh5! Qe7? (Diagram 11)

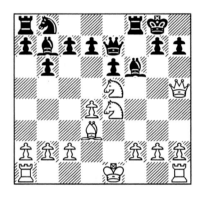

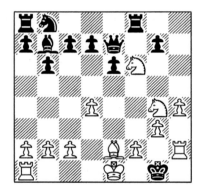

Diagram 11 (W)
A queen sacrifice is looming

Diagram 12 (W)
It really is on g1!

Losing at once. The right move was still 10...Bxe5!.

11 Qxh7+!!

The beginning of a marvellous king hunt.

11...Kxh7 12 Nxf6+ Kh6 13 Neg4+ Kg5 14 h4+ Kf4 15 g3+ Kf3 16 Be2+

Actually, there was an even quicker and more beautiful finish with 16 0-0!! when no matter what Black plays next move it will be 17 Nh2 mate.

16...Kg2 17 Rh2+ Kg1 (Diagram 12) 18 Kd2 mate (1-0)

This finish is given in most sources, but personally I find 18 0-0-0 mate more aesthetically pleasing.

If Black responds in passive style to 4 Bg5 then it is also possible for White to revert to the f2-f3 idea in an improved form, as the next game indicates.

Game 3
☐ **B.Lalic** ■ **V.Kovacevic**
Slavonski Brod 1995

1 d4 f5 2 e4 fxe4 3 Nc3 Nf6 4 Bg5 c6

Black's idea is that after 5 Bxf6?! exf6 6 Nxe4 d5 he has the two bishops and, more to the point, the white knight is evicted from e4. Handing over the bishop pair wouldn't necessarily have perturbed players such as Pillsbury and Chigorin who genuinely believed that knights were more valuable pieces than bishops. Indeed, the games of Emanuel Lasker seem to suggest that he too was over-partial to the knight. One of the first games that showed the value of the bishop pair was Neumann-Steinitz, Baden-Baden 1870, which continued 7 Ng3 Qb6 8 Qe2+ Kf7! 9 0-0-0 Na6 10 Qf3 g6 11 Bd3 Nb4 12 Kb1 h5! 13 h3 h4 14 Nge2 Nxd3 15 Rxd3 Bf5. Steinitz has pushed back the white knights, denying them centre squares, and now his bishops rule supreme. He finally managed to convert his advantage after 96(!) moves. If I may be allowed the digression, I first saw this game in a book by Euwe called *The Development of Chess Style* when I was a young boy and it instantly became my favourite game – its length and intricacies made a satisfying contrast to the bland diet of 'brilliant' 20-move wins to which I had hitherto been exposed in books written for beginners.

5 f3!

Naturally a strong, modern grandmaster like Bogdan Lalic isn't going to acquiesce to positional inferiority after only five moves as White.

5...exf3

The moment has gone for the idea of ...d7-d5 as after 5...d5 6 fxe4 dxe4 7 Bc4 White has a dangerous initiative. Compared to the 4 f3 d5 line discussed above, White has gained the useful attacking move Bg5 whilst Black has lost the ability to counterattack against d4 with ...Nc6 as his own pawn on c6 is blocking the square.

6 Nxf3 d5 7 Bd3 g6?

Too slow. It was imperative for Black to play 7...Bg4! in order to slow down White's attack and at the same time speed up his own development. Then 8 h3 Bxf3 9 Qxf3 Nbd7 10 0-0-0 Qa5 11 Rhe1 0-0-0 12 Bf5 **(Diagram 13)** is given as good for White in *Chess Informant*.

However, Black can escape from the bind with a precise sequence of moves given by your author on the *ChessPublishing.com* website, namely 12...g6! 13 Bxf6 Bh6+! 14 Kb1 exf6 15 Bxd7+ Rxd7 16 Qxf6 Rf8 17 Qe6 Qc7 and all danger has passed for Black.

TIP: In the Staunton, Black should always be looking for ways to hand back the pawn in order to relieve the pressure.

8 Ne5!

Shades of Lasker-Thomas. Black will soon regret he didn't lop off this knight when he had the chance.

8...Qb6

Black doesn't rate his chances of being able to resist the attack after 8...Bg7 9 Qe2 Nbd7 10 Nf3 0-0 11 h4! and so tries to confuse matters.

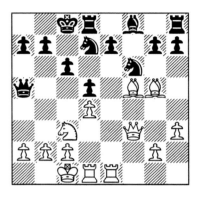

Diagram 13 (B)
Good for White?

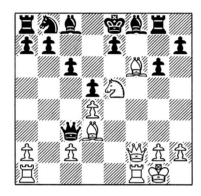

Diagram 14 (W)
Black's in real trouble

9 Qe2 Qxb2 10 0-0! Qxc3 11 Bxf6 Rg8 12 Qf2! (Diagram 14) 12...Nd7

There would be a massacre after 12...exf6 13 Qxf6 intending 14 Qf7+.

13 Bxe7! Kxe7 14 Nxd7 Kxd7 15 Qf7+ Be7 16 Qxg8 Qxd4+ 17 Kh1 Qh4 18 Rae1 Kd6 19 g3 Qg5 20 Qe8 d4 21 h4! Qd5+ 22 Kh2 1-0

The only way to fend off disaster on e7 is with 22...Be6, but then after 23 Qxa8 White has emerged from his attack two exchanges up.

Black answers 4 Bg5 with 4...Nc6!

It is now time to consider Black's best response to 4 Bg5, namely 4...Nc6! **(Diagram 15)**.

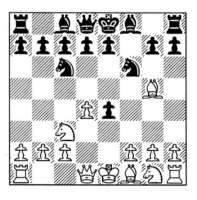

Diagram 15 (W)
4...Nc6 – the best response

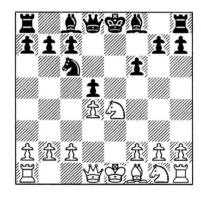

Diagram 16 (W)
Black has the bishop pair

The black knight attacks d4, which cannot be supported by the natural move Nf3 because of the black pawn on e4. If White plays 5 Bxf6 exf6 6 Nxe4 then after 6...d5 **(Diagram 16)** he has handed over the bishop pair for no profit.

Game 4
☐ **B.Hughey** ■ **K.Spraggett**
Winnipeg 2004

---

1 d4 f5 2 e4 fxe4 3 Nc3 Nf6 4 Bg5 Nc6 5 d5 Ne5 6 Qe2

The alternative move is 6 Qd4, attacking the black knight, but 6...Nf7! is a good reply, for example 7 Bh4 g5 8 Bg3 Bg7 and the black bishop is already on the 'Indian' diagonal; or 7 Bxf6 exf6 8 Nxe4 f5! (more energetic than 8...Be7 – again we want the bishop on g7!) 9 Ng3 g6 10 0-0-0 Bh6+ 11 Kb1 0-0 and Black is ready to realign the bishop with 12...Bg7, when he has a pleasant position. If instead 7 h4 then 7...c6! 8 0-0-0 Qb6 is an important challenge to the white queen. Black's centre holds firm after 9 Bxf6 gxf6 10 Qxe4 Qxf2 11 Nf3 Bh6+ 12 Kb1 Qe3 etc. when White is in trouble.

6...c6!

It is important that Black doesn't waste any time or else White will have the chance to castle queenside and then take on e4 with a fine game. Instead the white centre is going to be dissolved and replaced by black pawns.

7 0-0-0

Note that if 7 Bxf6 gxf6! Black doesn't get mated so he enjoys a broad, solid centre.

7...cxd5 8 Nxd5 e6! (Diagram 17)

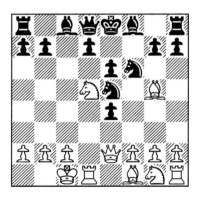

Diagram 17 (W)
Courageous play

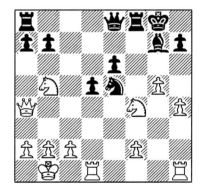

Diagram 18 (W)
The threats are looming

It takes some courage to play like this, but unless Black gets killed by an instant tactic he is making a lot of progress towards control of the centre.

WARNING: Don't be afraid of ghosts! Always play the moves you want to play unless you see a genuine tactical drawback.

9 Nc3 Nf7 10 Bxf6 gxf6! 11 Qxe4 f5

Black was also doing nicely after 11...Bh6+ 12 Kb1 f5 13 Qb4 Qe7 14 Qxe7+ Kxe7 15 Nf3 b6 16 Nd4 Bb7, when he had a strong centre to complement his bishop pair in Radjabov-Danielsen, Torshavn 2000.

12 Qa4 Bh6+ 13 Kb1 0-0

Black's centre is keeping White's knight out of the squares d5 and e4, while the bishop on f1 has little potential scope. Meanwhile Black has the makings of a strong attack against b2 once he retreats his bishop to g7 and starts advancing his queenside pawns. White tries to gain active play on the kingside, but Black's centre just gains in strength.

14 g4 f4 15 h4 Ne5 16 Nh3 d5 17 g5 Bg7 18 Nxf4

White wins a pawn, but Black is able to gain a huge number of tempi for his attack as the white queen is obliged to keep f4 defended.

18...Bd7 19 Bb5 Bxb5 20 Nxb5 Qe8! (Diagram 18)

With the threat of 21...Rxf4 or, even better, 21...a6!.

21 Nh3 a6 22 Nc3 b5 23 Qb4 Nc4 24 Rd3

Now White's queen gets into trouble, but it was already too late to save the game. The pressure against b2 exerted by the black knight and bishop was bound to prove fatal.

24...a5! 25 Qxb5 Na3+ 26 bxa3 Rb8 27 a4 Qc6 28 Kc1 Rxb5 29 axb5 Qc4 30 Kd2 Rc8 31 Ne2 Qxc2+ 32 Ke3 d4+ 33 Nxd4 Bxd4+ 34 Rxd4 Rc3+ 35 Kf4 Qf5 mate (0-1)

So Black extracts revenge for being mated in the Lasker game above. The conclusion is that the Staunton Gambit leads to lively and interesting play, but for Black as much as White.

White Plays 2 Bg5

Introduction

1 d4 f5 2 Bg5 (Diagram 1)

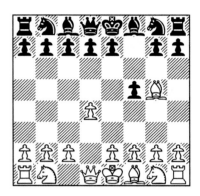 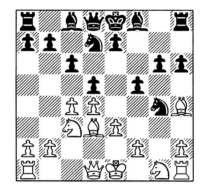

Diagram 1 (B)
White attacks the ghost of the f6-knight

Diagram 2 (W)
Spot the queen sacrifice!

If you are a Stonewall or Classical Dutch fan then 2 Bg5 is a rather annoying move. I don't need to tell you why 2...e6 is a bad reply (at least I hope not!) while after 2...Nf6?! 3 Bxf6 exf6 there is no Classical option and upon 4 e3 d5 5 c4 White has a definite opening advantage as the Stonewall set-up is being mangled.

Black could also set up a Stonewall with the more sensible 2...d5, but once again White can put quick pressure on the d5-square with c2-c4 or even start a kingside attack based on Bd3 and g2-g4, as he hasn't committed himself to a kingside fianchetto. Here is a drastic example which combined the two ideas: 1 d4 f5 2 Bg5 d5 3 e3 Nf6 4 c4 Nbd7?! 5 Nc3 h6?! 6 Bh4 g6 7 Bd3 c6 8 g4! Nxg4?? **(Diagram 2)** 9 Qxg4! and Black chose to be mated on h5 with 9...g5 10 Qh5 rather than on g6 after 9...fxg4 10 Bxg6 (Estoyanoff-Falco, Montevideo 1999).

Therefore, it is more promising for Black to go into a Leningrad-style set-up with 2...g6 or, in a more extreme form, with 2...h6!?. We'll start by looking at the latter move, which if nothing else sets some good traps!

Theoretical?

When 2 Bg5 is played by a member of the '2 Bg5 against everything' Trompowsky brigade, probably not; when it is played by Gary Kasparov, then yes! In particular, I would recommend you look at the sharp theory given below if you intend to respond with 2...h6.

Black's Maverick 2...h6

No doubt your first thought when you see this move is to wonder whether Black will end up being mated by Qh5 as in the miniature above. In fact, with this is mind, someone once tried 3 e3 in a tournament game, but found to his horror that after 3...hxg5 there was no mate! So White has to retreat his bishop: 3 Bh4, when there follows 3...g5 **(Diagram 3)**.

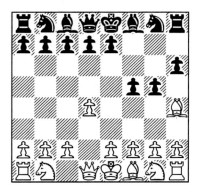

Diagram 3 (W)
Chasing the bishop

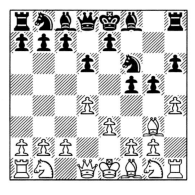

Diagram 4 (B)
Played by Kasparov

Black gains time to clear the way for ...Bg7, and has also carried out the pawn advance ...g7-g5, which is one of his favourite ideas in the Leningrad variation. The question is whether White can exploit this early loosening of the black kingside, as in the long-term Black's play has a lot to recommend it. White has two attempts that lead to sharp variations:

Firstly, 4 e4 Nf6! 5 Bg3 f4 6 e5 e6! – it is more important to free Black's game than take the bishop on g3 straightaway. After either 7 exf6 Qxf6 8 Nf3 Nc6 or 7 Bxf4 gxf4 8 exf6 Qxf6 9 Qh5+ Qf7 10 Qxf7+ Kxf7 Black will have dynamic chances based on ...Bg7.

Secondly, 4 e3 Nf6 5 Bg3 d6 6 h4! **(Diagram 4)** has been played by Kasparov.

Now 6...g4 closing the kingside looks like the best response, when if 7 Ne2 then 7...Nh5 8 Nf4 Nxf4 9 Bxf4 Bg7 intending ...e7-e5 is interesting, whilst I think the plan of 7...Be6!? 8 Nf4 Bf7 deserves attention, as the light-squared bishop is a sterling defender on f7.

Note that if 4 Bg3 then the greedy 4...f4? leads to disaster: 5 e3! e5 (or else Black loses a pawn to 6 exf4 in dealing with the mate threat on h5) 6 exf4 exf4 7 Qh5+ Ke7 8 Bxf4! gxf4 9 Qe5+ Kf7 10 Bc4+ Kg6 11 Qxh8 and Black is being annihilated. Instead Black should play 4...Nf6, when 5 e4 f4! 6 e5 e6 and 5 e3 d6 transpose to the two lines above.

So much for all the high-class theory. For braver souls, I have selected a game that reveals an objectively unsound, but highly tricky alternative for Black.

Game 5
☐ **D.Gormally** ■ **S.Zeidler**
Dyfed 1999

1 d4 f5 2 Bg5 h6 3 Bh4 c5?!

If you are feeling lucky then give this move a go. It sets a great trap as after the very plausible reply 4 dxc5? Black can win a piece with 4...Qa5+! 5 Nc3 g5 – there is no longer a mate on h5 after 6 Bg3 f4 7 e3 as the black queen has kindly vacated the d8-square. Therefore, Black can play 7...fxg3 with a clear conscience.

4 e3!

Upon 4 e4 it is annoying for Black that 4...Qa5+ 5 Nd2 g5 can be refuted by the simple 6 Qh5+ Kd8 7 Bxg5, so he has to fish in troubled waters with 4...Qb6 5 Nd2 cxd4 6 exf5 Nf6 7 Nb3 e5!?, when if 8 fxe6 then 8...Bb4+ is complex.

4...Qb6

Here is the second sneaky trap: this time 5 dxc5 apparently gives White a useful initiative after 5...Qxb2 6 Nd2, don't you agree? However, Black has 4...Qb4+! and the bishop on h4 is lost in a different way.

5 Nc3!

Danny Gormally, a player of grandmaster strength, doesn't easily fall for traps. Perhaps Black should have picked a more amenable opponent on which to practise his wiles?

5...cxd4 6 exd4 (Diagram 5)

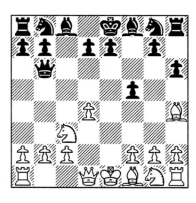

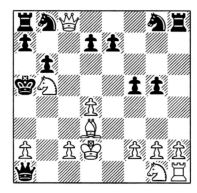

Diagram 5 (B)
A piece is on offer

Diagram 6 (W)
Black's monarch shouldn't survive

6...Qe6+

Black wins a piece after all, but the White attack proves overwhelming.

Norwegian GM Simen Agdestein had the following terrifying ordeal as Black against an amateur player rated 430 points below him: 6...g5 7 Qh5+ Kd8 8 Bxg5 Qxb2 9 Kd2 Qxa1 10 Qf7 hxg5 11 Qxf8+ Kc7 12 Nb5+ Kb6 13 Qd8+ Ka6 14 Bd3 b6 15 Qxc8+ Ka5 **(Diagram 6)**.

Now 16 Nc3! with the threat of 17 Qc4 and then mate on a4 or b5 wins easily, for example 16...Qb2 (what else?) 17 Qc4 Qb4 18 Qd5+ b5 19 a3! Qb2 20 Qxa8 and White is not only a piece up but he is about to make mincemeat of the black king's defences. Instead White played 16 Ne2 Nf6 17 Qc4 Qb2 and here he lost his nerve and went for the endgame with 18 Qb3? Qxb3 19 axb3 but only drew after 19...Ka6 20 Nc7+ Kb7 21 Nxa8 e6 22 Nxb6 axb6 – the grandmaster's technique was too good. Instead 18 Nbc3 still does the trick: 18...Qb4 19 Qxb4+ Kxb4 20 Rb1+ Ka5 21 Rb3! b5 – or else 22 Ra3+ Kb4 23 Ra4 mate – 22 Rxb5+ Ka6 23 Rxb8+ etc.

7 Be2 g5 8 Nf3!

Again it is worth considering whether the players you meet regularly in tournaments or club games would have not only the strategical skill to make this positional sacrifice, but also the tactical finesse to carry out the final attack. Or would they have panicked long before this point at the idea they were going to lose a piece?

8...gxh4 9 Ne5 Nf6 10 0-0 h5 11 Re1 Qb6 (Diagram 7)

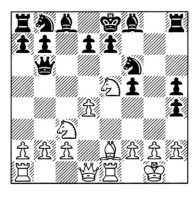

Diagram 7 (W)
11...Qb6: perhaps not the best

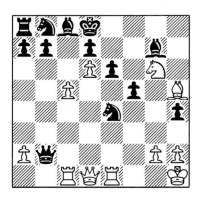

Diagram 8 (W)
Eliminate the knight on e4

It might have been worth throwing in 11...h3!? to try to confuse the issue with mate threats with the queen against g2 at a future point from c6 or g8. The game continuation allows an elegant riposte.

12 Nd5! Nxd5 13 Bxh5+ Kd8 14 Nf7+ Kc7 15 Nxh8 Bg7 16 Ng6

Black still has a nominal material advantage, but he wouldn't win any prizes for development or king safety.

16...e6 17 c4 Nf6 18 d5 Ne4 19 c5 Qxb2 20 d6+ Kd8 21 Rc1 Qxf2+
22 Kh1 Qb2 (Diagram 8) 23 Rxe4!

Leading to a brilliant finish, but then such things are always possible
when your opponent has his king in the centre and his queenside
pieces all lined up for the start of a new game.

23...fxe4 24 Qe1 Na6 25 Qxh4+ Bf6 26 Rf1! 1-0

The queen is immune due to mate on f8.

The Natural 2...g6

1 d4 f5 2 Bg5 g6 (Diagram 9)

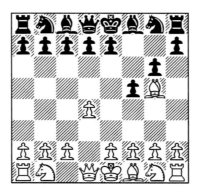

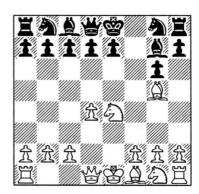

Diagram 9 (W)	Diagram 10 (B)
Black plays 2...g6	An unchallenged knight

Perhaps the most natural reply, especially if you play the Leningrad.
The drawback is that White can immediately break open the centre
after 3 Nd2 Bg7 (instead 3...d5 would be very risky, as after 4 c4
Black wouldn't be able to stabilise the Stonewall centre as he has
wasted time with 2...g6) 4 e4 fxe4 (4...Bxd4? 5 exf5 is too hazardous
for Black) 5 Nxe4 **(Diagram 10)**.

If you have read the first chapter you will be aware of what a nuisance an unchallenged White knight on e4 can be. If 5...Nf6?! then 6
Nxf6+ exf6 7 Be3!, intending to build up with Qd2, 0-0-0 and Bh6, is
very pleasant for White and lifeless for Black. So Black does best to
challenge the knight with 5...d5!, when White's best reply is 6 Nc5.
'What about the weaknesses left on e6 and e7?' you might well ask.
Well, there aren't going to be any weaknesses if Black's strategy succeeds: he is planning to transform the backward pawn on e7 into an
attacking weapon with ...e7-e5. It all depends on whether there is
enough dynamism in Black's set-up to carry the day; if not, White can
organise his pieces to control the e5-square and make Black pay for
loosening his pawn structure.

Game 6
□ **T.Nalbandian** ■ **V.Topalov**
Biel 1993

1 d4 f5 2 Bg5 g6 3 e4!? fxe4 4 Nc3 Bg7

If 4...d5 then 5 f3! gives White a good version of the Staunton Gambit. Black sensibly transposes into the 3 Nd2 Bg7 4 e4 fxe4 5 Nxe4 line.

5 Nxe4 d5 6 Nc5 b6

Black takes the chance to drive the white knight back into the wilderness on b3.

7 Nb3 Nh6!

Because Black suffered a quick defeat here, this move has been frowned upon. In fact, it is the frequent fate of a new idea that is judged by the outcome of a big-name game rather than its intrinsic merit. If Kasparov loses with a new move there is hardly any hope for it to gain acceptance, despite the fact that the move was the product of the most brilliant chess laboratory in the history of chess.

If we look beyond the bare statistics of '1-0, 22 moves' we can see a lot of worth in the wing development of the knight. Black intends to put it back on f7, where it not only attacks the white bishop on g5 but also joins in the fight for the key e5-square. Instead, after the routine 7...Nf6 White can gain a small but definite advantage: 8 Nf3 0-0 9 Be2 Ne4 10 Be3 etc.

8 h4

The most aggressive response. A more positional course is 8 Nf3!? Nf7 9 Bh4 0-0 10 Be2 Qd6 11 0-0 Nc6 (here 11...Bb7!? intending ...e7-e5 looks preferable) 12 c4! (breaking up Black's centre before he can play ...e7-e5 with effect) 12...Bg4 13 cxd5 Nb4 14 h3 Bf5 15 Rc1 Nxd5 and now 16 Bg3 looks slightly better for White. Instead, in Wells-McDonald, British League 2000 White played sharply to win but it rebounded: 16 Bb5?! Bh6! 17 Rc6 Qd8 18 Bc4 Nb4 19 Ne5 Nxc6 20 Nxc6 Qd6 21 Nxe7+ Kh8 22 Re1 Bd7 23 Nd5 Bg5! 24 Bxg5 Nxg5 25 Qd2 b5 26 Qxg5 bxc4 27 Re7 Rae8 28 Qh6. This looks crushing as if 28...Rxe7 then 29 Qxf8 mate, but after 28...Rf7! White had to resign as it will be mate on e1 if he takes the rook on f7.

8...Nf7 9 Nh3 Qd6 10 Qd2 e5?

This should wait. Before the game with Wells given in the last note I had studied the Topalov game and was ready to play 10...a5! here. **(Diagram 11)**.

If then 11 0-0-0? the reply 11...a4 12 Na1 a3 leaves the white knight on a ridiculous square on a1 and the white king vulnerable. So White should probably prefer 11 a4, but then the queenside is no longer an attractive haven for his king; perhaps 11...Bd7!? aiming straightaway at a4 is the best riposte.

Once White's king is deprived of shelter on the queenside, he can no longer carry out the smooth plan of attack seen in the game. Therefore, Black could prepare ...e7-e5 with dynamic play.

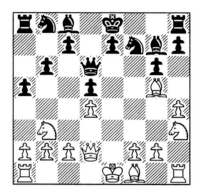

Diagram 11 (B)
11...a5 – an improvement

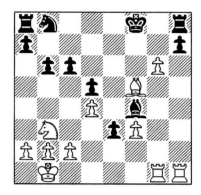

Diagram 12 (B)
The g-pawn is decisive

11 0-0-0 Nxg5 12 hxg5 e4 13 Qf4!

Topalov must have underestimated this move. Black has an impressive centre and the bishop pair, but he is a long way behind in development. Given time he would mobilise all his pieces in support of his centre, but everything now happens too quickly to give him any chance.

13...Bf8

If 13...Qxf4+ 14 Nxf4 c6 then 15 c4! breaks things open.

14 g3 c6 15 f3! Bxh3

Both 15...Qxf4+ 16 Nxf4 exf3 17 Nxg6 and 15...exf4 16 Re1+ are bad for Black.

16 Bxh3 Qxf4+ 17 gxf4 Bd6 18 f5 Bf4+

Black's kingside pieces are fighting gallantly, but they are getting no help from the rook on a8 or the knight on b8.

19 Kb1 gxf5 20 Bxf5 e3 21 Rdg1 Kf8 22 g6 1-0 (Diagram 12)

The passed pawn cannot be stopped without losing a rook.

White Delays Bg5

As well as 2 Bg5, White can delay putting the bishop on g5 for a move. For example, 1 d4 f5 2 Nf3 Nf6 3 Bg5 **(Diagram 13)**.

This is rather awkward for Black if he likes to fianchetto on g7. The line 3...g6 4 Bxf6 exf6 5 e3 d5 6 c4 Be6 **(Diagram 14)**, whilst not as bad as it appears at first glance for Black, is in any case a long way from being a typical Leningrad set-up. Therefore, 3...e6 looks like the best response, when White will probably invest the bishop pair in order to free his game with the e2-e4 advance, as in the game below.

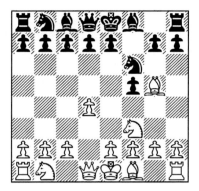

Diagram 13 (B)
A delayed Bg5

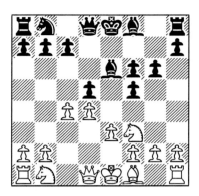

Diagram 14 (W)
Not bad but not ideal

Game 7
□ **C.Duncan** ■ **N.McDonald**
London 1998

**1 d4 f5 2 Nf3 Nf6 3 Bg5 e6 4 Nbd2 Be7 5 Bxf6 Bxf6 6 e4 0-0!
(Diagram 15)**

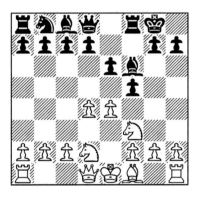

Diagram 15 (W)
6...0-0!

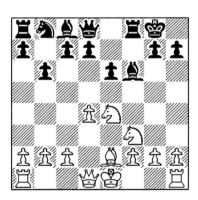

Diagram 16 (W)
Time to admit the mistake?

Black should avoid the obvious 6...fxe4, which just lets the white knight get to a strong square after 7 Nxe4. If you aren't convinced, then have a look back at Game 2.

7 Be2

A little bit passive. After the more direct 7 Bd3, 7...d5! refuses to concede space in the centre. Another one of my games then went 8 exf5 exf5 9 0-0 Nc6 10 c3 Qd6 11 Re1 a6 12 b4 g5!? with a nicely active position for Black in Kirsanov-McDonald, London 2001. Alas, chess is one long regret: if only I had remembered to take my opponent's queen in that game...

I can't resist showing you the following little game, even though it was played in a blitz tournament (in fact, the two protagonists probably play better with five minutes on the clock than most of us do with two hours!): 7 Bd3 g6?! 8 Qe2 Bg7? 9 c3 Nc6 (contrary to my claim of the previous note, I hope once you have read this chapter you will play better than Topalov here; he should have challenged the white centre with ...d7-d5 by now, and been ready to answer the blocking e4-e5 with ...c7-c5: a strategical necessity that vanishes once the knight goes to c6) 10 0-0-0 d5 11 e5! b6 12 h4! h6 13 Rdg1 Ne7 14 g4 f4 15 h5 g5. So it seems that Black has blocked the kingside and is ready at last for ...c7-c5. Of course, a strategical genius like Karpov would never have allowed his kingside attack to reach a dead end, even in a blitz game, and sure enough there followed 16 Nxg5! hxg5 17 h6 Bh8 18 Nf3 c5 (or 18...Nc6 19 Rh5) 19 Nxg5 cxd4 20 Bh7 mate.

7...fxe4

Here 7...d5 was the obvious response in view of what has been said above; but I was convinced my opponent had committed a criminal act with 7 Be2 and blocking the centre didn't seem to be the way to punish him. Therefore, I elected to play more sharply by capturing on e4 and then putting the queen's bishop on b7.

On the other hand, it is a moot point whether the slow 7 Be2 is any greater a sin against chess strategy than the supposed retribution 7...fxe4, which after all gives up the centre. In effect Black is trying to punish a positional mistake by making a positional mistake of his own! Here the position remains unclear, but it is worth remembering that trying too hard to take advantage of an error can lead to disaster. Be happy that your opponent is showing signs of fallibility or declining to set you problems with the sharpest moves, but don't be overeager to force the issue. Even in this age of rapid time controls, patience is still a virtue.

8 Nxe4 b6 (Diagram 16) 9 Qd2

Instead White could have admitted he had lost a tempo with 9 Bd3!? Bb7 10 Qe2 when he has a familiar centre build-up. However, Black can use his extra move to good effect with 10...c5!? when he has an impressive central pawn mass after 11 dxc5 bxc5!?. One important point is that 12 Nxc5?? Qa5+ wins a piece.

9...Bb7 10 Nxf6+ Qxf6 11 0-0-0 Nc6 12 Rhe1 Ne7 13 Ne5 Rad8 14 Bf3?!

White has no luck with this bishop. His last chance to play actively was with 14 Bb5!, attacking d7, when after 14...c6 15 Bc4 the black bishop is shut in and 15...Qxf2? fails tactically to 16 Nxd7! Rxd7 17 Bxe6+. Instead 15...Nd5 16 f3!? looks unclear.

14...Bxf3 15 Nxf3 Nd5

Suddenly Black has an excellent position with a safe centre, pressure along the f-file and the chance to play actively on the queenside.

16 Rf1 b5! (Diagram 17)

Diagram 17 (W)
Cementing the knight on d5

Diagram 18 (W)
With nasty threats

An important move that cements the knight on d5 as a prelude to an all-out attack on the queenside. White is unable to drum up any significant counterplay.

17 Ne5 c5! 18 g3 c4 19 c3 b4 20 Kb1

20 cxb4 c3 21 bxc3 Nxc3 22 Qxc3 Rc8 23 Nc4 d5 is horrid for White.

20...bxc3 21 bxc3 d6 22 Nxc4 Rc8 23 Nxd6 Rc6 24 c4 Rb8+ 25 Ka1 Nb4 (Diagram 18)

With the threat of 26...Qxd4+! 27 Qxd4 Nc2 mate.

26 a3 Ra6 27 Ne4 Qxd4+! 28 Qxd4 Nc2+ 29 Ka2 Rxa3 mate (0-1)

It is curious how often games in the Dutch end in mate rather than one player resigning!

Chapter Three

White Plays 2 Nc3

Introduction

1 d4 f5 2 Nc3 (Diagram 1)

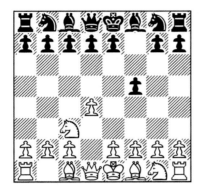

Diagram 1 (B)
White plays 2 Nc3

Diagram 2 (B)
A powerful bishop on f4

The early knight development carries the immediate positional threat of 3 e4 fxe4 4 Nxe4, when White has conquered space in the centre. Therefore 2...d5 or 2...Nf6 are the only logical replies.

Theoretical?

Not really. White wants a quiet situation in the centre so that he can manoeuvre on the wings. Finding the right plan is therefore more important than knowing a specific series of moves.

Black Plays 2...d5

Generally speaking, it makes sense to set up a Stonewall centre as the knight on c3 is blocking the move c2-c4, which in Queen's Pawn openings is the deadly foe of a black pawn on d5. If Black could follow up in the future with ...e7-e5, or else ...e7-e6 and then ...c7-c5, his pawns might have the greater share of the centre. However, Nemesis awaits Black in the form of White's dark squared bishop after 3 Bf4! **(Diagram 2)**. Here the bishop is on an excellent square: it surveys the hole on e5 and the weakened f4-b8 diagonal in general. It is a menace to the black queenside, but if it is challenged with ...Bd6, as it needs must be, the exchange of bishops leaves Black weak on the dark squares.

Game 8
☐ **V.Eingorn** ■ **V.Malaniuk**
Pocztowy 2000

1 d4 f5 2 Nc3 d5 3 Bf4 e6 4 e3 Nf6 5 Nf3 Bd6 (Diagram 3)

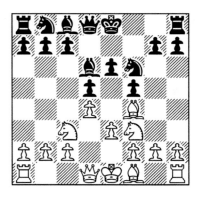

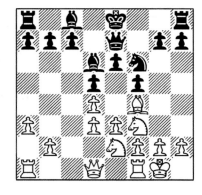

Diagram 3 (W)
Challenging the bishop on f4

Diagram 4 (B)
A change of structure

An alternative plan is to try for ...c7-c5, but it is problematical. For example, 5...a6 6 Bd3 c5 7 Ne5 Nc6 8 0-0 Be7 9 b3! (preventing ...c5-c4 as a prelude to his plan of winning control of the c5-square) 9...0-0 10 Nxc6 bxc6 11 Na4! (now Black will be obliged to allow the opening of the e-file with ...c5xd4) 11...Nd7 12 f3 cxd4 13 exd4 Bf6 14 c3 e5 15 dxe5 Nxe5 16 Re1! Nxd3 17 Qxd3 Ra7 18 Be5! (forcing off Black's dark-squared bishop to accentuate the weakness of c5 and d4) 18...Re7 19 Bxf6 Rxf6 20 Nc5 and White's knight dominated the dark squares, Ljubicic-Zelic, Split 2000.

6 Bd3 Nc6 7 0-0

Black has a solid-looking set-up, but what can he do? The only active plan is the attempt to break out with ...e6-e5, but this is always fraught with danger. In the same tournament as the main game, Emanuel Berg, a GM and Dutch expert, met 7 a3 with 7...Qe7 8 0-0 0-0 9 Nb5 e5? and there followed 10 dxe5 Bxe5 11 c4! Bxf4 12 exf4 Be6 (Malakhatko-Berg, Pocztowy 2000). If White had now found 13 Ng5! then Black would have had no good answer to the threat of 14 Nxe6 Qxe6 15 Nxc7, for if 13...dxc4 then 14 Nxc7! Rad8 15 Ncxe6 Rxd3 16 Qc2 looks horrible for Black.

7...Qe7 8 Ne2 Nb4

Understandably Black didn't much like the look of 8...e5 9 dxe5 Nxe5 10 Nxe5 Bxe5 11 c4!, with a similar initiative for White as in the Berg extract above. Nevertheless, the game continuation leaves him slowly being worn down along the c-file.

9 a3 Nxd3 10 cxd3! (Diagram 4)

TIP: Always be on the lookout for ways to change the pawn structure to your advantage.

10...0-0 11 Rc1

White has the semi open c-file on which to base his winning strategy.

It wouldn't mean much if Black had a counterattack on the kingside in full swing; in fact just a little activity somewhere (anywhere!) might be enough to throw White's plans off course. But here Black can do nothing at all to disturb his opponent.

11...b6 12 Rc3 Bb7 13 Qc2 Rfc8 14 Rc1 c6 15 Bxd6 Qxd6 16 b4 Nd7 17 Qb2 a5 18 b5

Finally a breach is forced in Black's wall of queenside pawns.

18...cxb5 19 Qxb5 (Diagram 5)

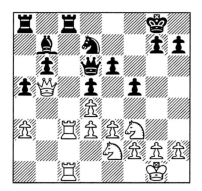

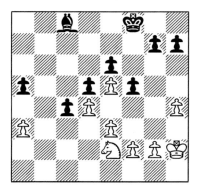

| **Diagram 5 (B)** | **Diagram 6 (B)** |
| A poor bishop on b7 | Good knight, bad bishop |

In normal circumstances the exchanges that now take place would help to free Black's position, but here they accentuate the weakness of the bad bishop on b7.

19...Rxc3 20 Rxc3 Rc8 21 Rxc8+ Bxc8 22 h4! Kf8

White wins easily after 22...Qxa3 23 Qc6 Qf8 24 Qxe6+ Qf7 25 Qc6, attacking the bishop and with ideas of 26 Ng5.

23 Ne5! Nxe5 24 dxe5 Qc5

Black has a horrid position after 24...Qxe5 25 Qxb6, but the endgame will be just as ghastly.

25 Qxc5+ bxc5 26 d4! c4 27 Kh2 (Diagram 6)

Now Black can do nothing as long as White keeps the c3-square guarded. The rest is a classic example of the knight versus bad bishop endgame which gives Stonewall Dutch players nightmares.

27...g6 28 Kg3 h6 29 Kf4 Bd7 30 Nc3 Bc6 31 g4 Ke7 32 g5 h5 33 Kf3 Kd8 34 Ke2 Kc7 35 Kd2 Be8 36 f3 Kc6 37 e4 fxe4 38 fxe4 Bf7 39 Ke3 Kd7 40 Nb5 Bg8 41 Nd6 Kc6 42 Kd2 Kb6 43 Nc8+ Kc7 44 Ne7 Bf7 45 exd5 exd5 46 e6 Bxe6 47 Nxg6 Kd6 48 Nf4 Bg4 49 g6 1-0

TIP: I would strongly recommend Black playing 2...Nf6, as after 2...d5 he faces a thankless defensive task, with few winning chances.

Black Plays 2...Nf6

In contrast to the section above, after 2...Nf6, the reply 3 Bf4? misses the mark completely, as there is no weakness along the diagonal for the bishop to exploit. On the contrary, it becomes a target, as Black can build up in Leningrad style with the aim of eventually harassing the white bishop with ...d7-d6 and ...e7-e5.

So after 2...Nf6, White should play 3 Bg5 when 3...d5 (how else to keep a hold on the centre?) 4 Bxf6 exf6 breaks up Black's pawns. Or rather, it is more accurate to say White removes the dynamism from Black's pawn centre. It will remain more or less fixed as there is no longer the chance to expand with ...e7-e5. White can either try for positional pressure on d5 by arranging c2-c4, or else, if Black castles queenside, he might launch a direct attack throwing forwards the queenside pawns. These two plans are often interconnected.

Still, the good news is that Black gets chances to play for a win here.

Game 9
☐ **I.Argandona Rivero** ■ **O.De la Riva Aguado**
Andorra 2002

1 d4 f5 2 Nc3 Nf6 3 Bg5 d5 4 Bxf6 exf6 5 e3 Be6 (Diagram 7)

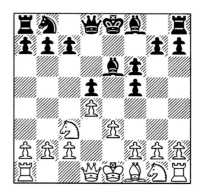 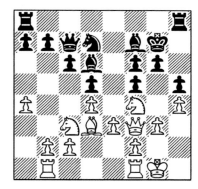

Diagram 7 (W)	**Diagram 8 (B)**
Delaying ...Nc6	Black uncorks a stunner!

Black mustn't play ...Nc6 until White has committed himself to Bd3, as if 5...Nc6 then 6 Bb5 is awkward. Black may well want to castle queenside, so he doesn't want his pawns there wrecked by Bxc6+.

6 Bd3

White has also tried 6 Bb5+, based on the principle that after 6...c6 the black knight on b8 is denied its rightful post on c6. Still, can it really be of benefit to White to spend a tempo persuading Black to play such a natural move? After 6...c6 there followed 7 Bd3 Qb6 8 Rb1

Nd7 9 Qf3 g6 10 Nge2 Bd6 11 a3 Qc7 12 h4 h5 13 Nf4 Bf7 14 g3 Kf8!
(Black has astutely delayed castling queenside and here he gives up
on it all together, and he's quite right to when White's pieces are
ready to sound the charge after 14...0-0-0 15 b4!) 15 0-0 Kg7 16 a4
(Diagram 8).

Here Malaniuk uncorked the great move 16...Ne5!!, which restores to
the black centre the energy that was removed from it with 4 Bxf6
exf6. After 17 dxe5 fxe5 18 Ng2 e4 19 Qd1 exd3 20 cxd3 d4! 21 exd4
Rad8 Black soon regained his pawn on d4, and the two bishops led
him to victory in Ulibin-Malaniuk, Pocztowy 2001.

6...Qd7 7 Qf3?!

White appears to want to do something active on the kingside, but
next move he changes his mind and decides on a queenside attack.
Nevertheless, after 7 Nge2 Nc6 8 Bb5 0-0-0 9 Nf4 Bf7 10 Qd2 Qd6 11
Bxc6 Qxc6 12 a3 g5 13 Nd3 f4! 14 0-0-0 fxe3 15 fxe3 Re8 16 h4 Bh6!
17 hxg5 Bxg5 Black had fully activated his game in Anastasian-
Dzhumaev, Linares 2000.

7...Nc6 8 a3?

The natural follow up to his previous move was 8 Nge2, aiming for
Nf4, h2-h4 etc.

**TIP: Once you decide on a plan you should try to carry it out unless
you see something clearly wrong with it. Chopping and changing
your ideas can lead to disaster.**

**8...0-0-0 9 Nge2 Kb8 10 Bb5 g5 11 g3 Qd6 12 Bxc6 Qxc6 13 Kd2
Be7 14 h4 Qd7 15 b4 b6 16 Rhb1 (Diagram 9)**

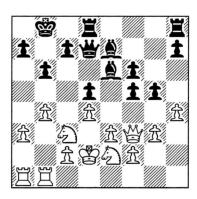

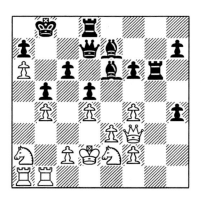

Diagram 9 (B)	**Diagram 10 (W)**
An offside queen on f3	The kingside is Black's

White continues his build up, but what on earth is the white queen
doing on f3? She should be on d3 or somewhere else on the queenside,
where she joins in the assault.

16...Rhg8 17 a4 f4!

The black attack in the centre proves more potent than White's action on the queenside.

TIP: If you are facing an attack on the wing, try to break open lines in the centre.

18 gxf4

White preserves the fortress around his king, but at the cost of conceding a tremendous outside passed pawn to his opponent.

18...gxh4 19 a5?

Strategically speaking, this is suicidal. White had to play 19 b5 first and only then 20 a5 to prevent Black's reply. The white attack would remain far from convincing, but that was far more preferable to being as dead as a doornail.

19...b5!

A weird-looking move, but what does that matter if it prevents lines becoming open on the queenside? The white rooks are now lined up on the a- and b-files for the grand assault but there is no way to get through.

20 a6 c6 21 Na2 Rg6 (Diagram 10)

Meanwhile, the black queen and rooks have no trouble in finding an inroad into White's position. White's pieces flounder around helplessly until Black decides to put him out of his misery.

22 Rg1 Rdg8 23 Qh5 h3 24 c3 Bd6 25 Ng3 Bg4 26 Qh4 Qg7 27 Nf1 f5 28 Re1 Be7 29 Qg3 Bh5 30 Qxh3 Rxg1 31 Qxh5 Qg2 32 Ke2 Qe4 33 Nd2 Rxe1+ 34 Kxe1 Qd3 35 Qh2 h5 36 Kd1 h4 37 Qh1 h3 38 Nc1 Qxc3 39 Ke2 Rh8 40 Qg1 h2 41 Qg7 h1Q 42 Qe5+ Kc8 0-1

Game 10
□ **R.Bagirov** ■ **M.Dzhumaev**
Abu Dhabi 2002

1 d4 f5 2 Nc3 Nf6 3 Bg5 d5 4 e3 (Diagram 11)

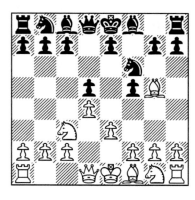

Diagram 11 (B)
The flexible 4 e3

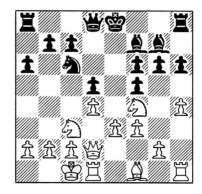

Diagram 12 (W)
11...exf6!

A slightly more flexible approach to the position than 4 Bxf6 above. White can also try 4 f3, hoping to expand in the centre with 5 e4. But 4...Nc6! is as good a response here as in the Staunton Gambit. It attacks the d4 pawn in an X-ray through its own d5-pawn. Black has a secure position after, say, 5 Qd2 e6 6 e3 Be7 7 Bb5 Bd7.

4...Be6!?

This is a common theme in the Stonewall centre where Black hasn't committed himself to ...e7-e6. The bishop is manoeuvred to f7, where it helps bolster both the d5-square and the kingside in general, and has the chance in some lines of becoming active on h5.

5 Nge2 Bf7 6 f3 Nc6 7 Nf4 a6!

An important move: Black prevents 8 Bb5, which would not only threaten to break up the black queenside pawns but also lessen Black's control over e5 by eliminating the knight.

8 Qd2 g6

So Black gets to play a kingside fianchetto after all.

9 0-0-0 Bg7 10 h4 h6 11 Bxf6 exf6! (Diagram 12)

An excellent decision. Black puts a guard on the e5-square, clears the e7-square for his knight and increases the size of the defensive clump of pawns on the kingside.

12 g4 fxg4 13 fxg4 Ne7 14 e4 dxe4 15 Nxe4 g5!

This move would have been suicidal if Black hadn't had the foresight to station his light-squared bishop on f7. The position is very double-edged, but it seems that Dzhumaev is right to trust in the strength of the dark-squared bishop on g7.

16 Nh5 Bxh5 17 gxh5 Qd5 18 Nc3 Qf7 19 Bh3 g4! (Diagram 13)

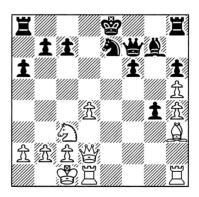
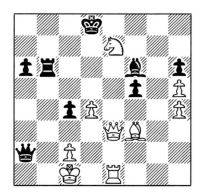

Diagram 13 (W)	**Diagram 14 (B)**
Activating the bishop	White has blundered

Another fine positional move. Black hands over a pawn in order to activate his bishop and secure the right to castle queenside.

20 Bxg4 f5 21 Bf3 0-0-0 22 Qf4 Rd6 23 Rd3 Rhd8 24 Rhd1 Qc4 25 Qe3 R8d7

Black now has full compensation for the pawn deficit in view of the enormous pressure he is exerting on d4.

26 b3 Qb4 27 Ne2 Qa3+ 28 Kb1 c5! 29 b4!?

A wild struggle now develops with both kings looking to be in deep trouble.

29...Qxb4+ 30 Rb3 Qa5 31 Bxb7+ Kd8 32 Bf3 c4 33 Rb8+ Kc7 34 Rb2 Nc8 35 Nf4 Re7 36 Rb7+ Kd8 37 Rxe7 Rb6+ 38 Kc1 Nxe7 39 Re1 Bf6 40 Ng6 Qxa2 41 Nxe7? (Diagram 14)

A losing blunder. Instead 41 Kd2! was unclear.

41...Rb1+ 42 Kd2 Qa5+ 43 Qc3 Qxc3+ 44 Kxc3 Rxe1 45 Nd5 Bxh4 46 Kxc4 Rf1 47 Be2 Rf2 48 Kd3 f4 49 c4 f3 50 Bd1 a5 51 Ke3 a4 52 Bxf3 a3 53 c5 Rxf3+ 0-1

Chapter Four

The Stonewall Dutch

Introduction

1 d4 f5 2 g3 Nf6 3 Bg2 e6 4 Nf3 d5 5 c4 c6 6 0-0 Bd6 (Diagram 1)

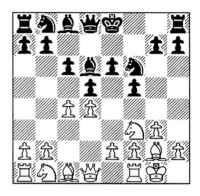

Diagram 1 (W)
A standard Dutch Stonewall position

Diagram 2 (W)
Another Stonewall

The word stonewall refers to a particular type of pawn centre rather than a fixed series of moves. In the Dutch, it describes a scenario in which Black puts pawns on d5, e6 and f5 and usually c6. These lock the centre very firmly and make it hard for White to undertake any action there. Black's structure is tough and resilient and almost immoveable, just like the Confederate general Thomas Jackson during the American Civil War, who became forever known as 'Stonewall' Jackson.

The Stonewall structure was used with great effect by the sixth world champion Mikhail Botvinnik, who passed on his knowledge of it to his pupil Vladimir Kramnik (the 14th world champion). It was also a favourite of Botvinnik's great rival David Bronstein.

It's best feature is that Black has a lovely grip on the light squares in the centre, in contrast to the other lines of the Dutch, where White is presented with a space advantage free of charge.

Move Order

As you will see from the illustrative games in this chapter, there are all sorts of ways to arrive at a Stonewall centre. Play could even begin 1 d4 d5 2 Nf3 e6 3 c4 f5. Or Black might adopt a Classical set-up and then throw in ...d7-d5; for example, a common method is 1 d4 f5 2 g3 Nf6 3 Bg2 e6 4 c4 Be7 5 Nf3 0-0 6 0-0 Ne4 7 Qc2 Bf6 8 Nc3 d5. The Stonewall centre also makes an appearance in all sorts of Dutch sidelines: two examples are 1 d4 f5 2 Nc3 d5 3 Nf3 Nf6 4 g3 c6 5 Bg2 e6 and 1 d4 f5 2 Bg5 g6 3 Nc3 d5 4 e3 Bg7 5 h4 c6 **(Diagram 2)**.

The latter example isn't strictly a Stonewall, as Black hasn't played ...e7-e6 (and a good job too!): but I can assure you that no one will laugh at you if you describe this as a Stonewall centre. In fact, any position with black pawns on d5 and f5, separated by a backward pawn on e7 or e6, with a hole on e5, is commonly regarded as a Stonewall.

 WARNING: Even if you intend to play the Leningrad or Classical, don't skip this chapter. You cannot hope to play the Dutch properly unless you have some idea of how to handle the Stonewall structure.

Theoretical?

No. The fact that Black blocks the centre with pawns greatly reduces the number of forcing, attacking variations available to White. Therefore the instant clash of arms that tends to generate long theoretical struggles is avoided.

Black's Kingside Attack against Passive Play

We'll start by examining what Black can achieve in the Stonewall if he plays in direct, attacking style and meets with no resistance. If you intend to play like this as Black, I advise you to enjoy the fair weather of the first few games, as there will be some storms ahead!

Game 11
□ **H.Birkholz** ■ **P.Harzer**
Schkopau 1954

1 d4 e6 2 c4 f5 3 g3 Nf6 4 Bg2 d5 5 Nf3 c6 6 0-0 Bd6 7 b3 Nbd7 8 Bb2

Having clogged up the centre with pawns, Black now starts an attack of breathtaking artlessness: stick the knight on e4, put the queen on f6, batter open the h-file, get the queen in front of the rook along the h-file, and then mate on h2. He gets to carry out this plan in its entirety, except that the mate occurs with the queen on h3, not h2...

8...Ne4 9 Nbd2 Qf6 10 Ne1

White clears the way for f2-f3 to evict the knight from e4, but it only encourages Black's next move. Though I doubt if leaving the knight on f3 would have dissuaded him: 10 Qc2 h5 11 Rad1 h4 12 Nxh4 g5 as in the game.

10...h5! (Diagram 3)

Here we go: if now 11 h4 then 11...g5! and the pawns keep on coming at the white king.

11 Ndf3

A panicky reaction, but it is too late for a counterattack in the centre: 11 f3 Nxd2 (but not 11...Ng5 12 e4!) 12 Qxd2 h4 13 e4 hxg3 14 e5

Nxe5! 15 dxe5 Bc5+ 16 Bd4 Qh4! with the double threat of mate on h2 and 17...Bxd4+.

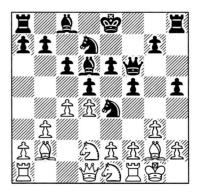

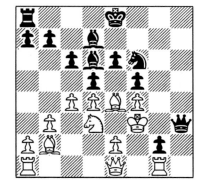

Diagram 3 (W)
Crude but effective

Diagram 4 (W)
A good advert for the Stonewall

11...h4 12 Nxh4 g5!

This is better than the immediate 12...Rxh4? 13 gxh4, answering 13...Qxh4 with 14 Nf3. Hence Black aims to get the g-pawn to g4 in order to prevent the defence Nf3.

13 Nhf3 g4 14 Nh4 Rxh4! 15 gxh4 Qxh4 16 f4 Ndf6

Unfortunately for a man in a hurry, if 16...gxf3 then 17 Nxf3 defends h2. Therefore Black needs to bring the rook sitting on a8 into the attack with the moves ...Ndf6, ...Bd7, ...0-0-0 and ...Rh8. This seems painfully slow, but what exactly can White do in the meantime? It would take all the pieces to fall off the board in an earthquake to distract Black from his plan. That is the beauty of the Stonewall: if White plays passively and fails to make a dent on the black centre or on the queenside he can be completely overrun.

17 Nd3 Bd7 18 Qe1 Qh5 19 h4

Falling apart, but White was understandably terrified about 19...0-0-0 and 20...Rh8 with butchery to follow on the h2-square.

19...g3 20 Bxe4 Qxh4 21 Kg2 Qh2+ 22 Kf3 g2 23 Rg1 Qh3+ 0-1 (Diagram 4)

24 Qg3 dxe4+ 25 Kf2 Ng4+ wins the white queen, while 24 Kf2 Ng4 is mate – more elegant than 24...Nxe4 mate.

Back in the 1930s, the young Botvinnik crushed positionally naïve but world-class players with a rustic form of the Stonewall: do your regular opponents play better chess than grandmasters of that era? If not, then the Stonewall in its direct, attacking form could be for you.

NOTE: Sophisticated? No. Effective? Yes! At most levels the Stonewall is easier to play as Black than as White.

Game 12
☐ **H.Steiner** ■ **M.Botvinnik**
Groningen 1946

1 d4 e6 2 c4 f5 3 g3 Nf6 4 Bg2 Bb4+ 5 Bd2 Be7 6 Nc3 0-0 7 Qc2?! (Diagram 5)

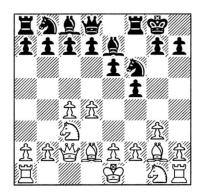

Diagram 5 (B)
7 Qc2: natural but dubious

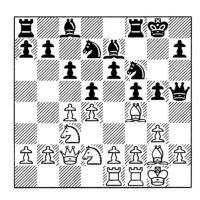

Diagram 6 (W)
12...g7-g5!

A natural move, as it stops 7...Ne4 and has ideas of e2-e4, but in fact it does more harm than good as the queen is poorly placed on c2. Instead 7 Nf3 d5 8 0-0 c6 9 a3!? Qe8 10 b4 to gain space on the queenside was a better approach.

Note that after 7 Nf3, the reply 7...Ne4 was possible but Steiner had no reason to want to go to the trouble of misplacing his queen on c2 in order to prevent it. For example, 8 0-0 Bf6 9 Nxe4 fxe4 9 Ne5 is a good, active response by White. Furthermore, if 8 0-0 Nxd2? Black gains the bishop pair but he has wasted a lot of time: and wasn't the purpose of the opening to prove the white bishop was badly placed on d2, rather than to exchange it off?

7...d5!

Stopping e2-e4 and entering a favourable Stonewall.

8 Nf3 c6 9 0-0 Qe8 10 Bf4

It is becoming clear that White has no idea of how to handle the position. A couple of years after this game, Flohr came up with a clever idea to be rid of his bad bishop on d2 for its more precious counterpart on e7: 10 a3 Qh5 11 Na2 Nbd7 12 Bb4 Re8 13 Bxe7 Rxe7 14 Nb4 with interesting play in Flohr-Szabo, Budapest 1949.

10...Qh5 11 Rae1

Here 11 Bxb8 might have been the best way to bail out because the bishop becomes a target.

11...Nbd7 12 Nd2

White clears the way for f2-f3 and e2-e4: a logical positional plan, but he has missed the strength of Black's reply.

12...g5! (Diagram 6)

Here the circumstances are perfect for this pawn thrust: White has no discernible counterplay anywhere; it comes with gain of time; and the bishop on f4 is fatally short of squares.

13 Bc7 Ne8 14 Be5 Nxe5 15 dxe5 f4 16 gxf4

Opening up the g-file is suicidal, but otherwise White can only sit and watch as Black slowly builds up his attack.

16...gxf4 17 Nf3 Kh8 18 Kh1 Ng7 19 Qc1 Bd7 20 a3 Rf7 21 b4 Rg8 22 Rg1 Nf5! 23 Nd1 (Diagram 7)

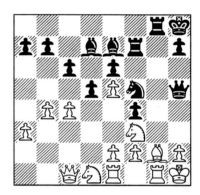

Diagram 7 (B)
White is terribly passive

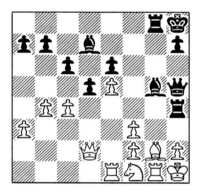

Diagram 8 (W)
...Bf4 is coming

After 23 Qxf4 Black could win the queen by checking on g3, but 23...Rg4 as in the game looks even stronger.

23...Rfg7 24 Qxf4 Rg4 25 Qd2 Nh4 26 Ne3

Of course after 26 Nxh4 Rxh4, mate will follow on the h-file.

26...Nxf3 27 exf3 Rh4 28 Nf1 Bg5 0-1 (Diagram 8)

Black's attack reaches its completion after 29...Bf4 when h2 is indefensible. This was a good demonstration of Black's chances, though White's resistance was very feeble.

An obvious way for White to meet Black's plan of a kingside attack is by breaking open the centre with the moves f2-f3 and e2-e4. If this plan were strong and easy to carry out, then the Stonewall would long have ceased to exist as a respectable opening. It would no doubt have been reduced to rubble by Rubinstein or Capablanca in a couple of famous games back in the 1920s and then ceased to be anything more than a historical curiosity.

Fortunately for Stonewall fans, the moves f2-f3 and e2-e4 are not only difficult to arrange, but they also create weaknesses in the white camp and notably deprive the white knight of the f3-square, which can only make the kingside less well defended. As we saw in the game above, Steiner's attempt to advance e2-e4 was doomed.

Here follows an even more spectacular failure by White from the early days of the Stonewall. After the sequence ...Ne4, Nxe4, ...f5xe4 White can try to break open lines and dissolve the strong pawn on e4 with f2-f3. However, this move is almost always double-edged, as it weakens the white kingside. In the following example it backfires completely.

Game 13
☐ **E.Grünfeld** ■ **C.Torre Repetto**
Baden-Baden 1925

1 d4 e6 2 Nf3 f5 3 g3 Nf6 4 Bg2 d5 5 0-0 Bd6 6 c4 c6 7 Qc2 0-0 8 b3 Ne4 9 Bb2 Nd7 10 Ne5 Qf6 (Diagram 9)

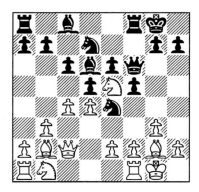

Diagram 9 (W)	**Diagram 10 (W)**
Typical Stonewall play by Black	White will be mated

Here White decided it was the moment to challenge the black knight as a prelude to future expansion with e2-e4, but it all went horribly wrong:

11 f3 Nxe5! 12 dxe5??

The weakness created on the a7-g1 diagonal is decisive. If instead 12 fxe4, it is the hole on e3 that is White's undoing: 12...Ng4! 13 e5 Qh6 (threatening mate on h2) 14 h3 Ne3.

The only chance was 12 c5! as it blocks the c5-square and leaves three black pieces hanging. But even here Black can manoeuvre so that he gains control of a key centre square: 12...Nf7!? 13 fxe4 Bc7. Then Black is ready to play ...Ng5, no matter what White decides to do with his e4-pawn, when a second black knight is poised to land on e4. And this time there will be no white pawn available to dislodge it.

You will see how a weakening pawn move can have direct or indirect repercussions. In the last variation, there is a ripple out effect so that e4 becomes a weakness. The fact that White had to play 12 c5 rather than recapturing gave Black a flexibility in the choice of piece to be kept on the board: he could therefore choose to save the knight on e5 and head it towards e4.

Still, this was infinitely preferable to what happens in the game – the shortest defeat of Grünfeld's chess career.

12...Bc5+ 13 Kh1 Nxg3+! 0-1 (Diagram 10)

White has to resign as he will be mated after 14 hxg3 Qh6+.

Positional Considerations

So far Black has had everything his own way. Now it is time to look at some examples from modern chess in which White gets his strategy right. First, we should consider the positional deficiencies of the Stonewall on which White can hope to build a successful plan.

Positional Drawbacks of the Stonewall

There are three main drawbacks to the Stonewall. Firstly, assuming Black plays ...c7-c6 to bolster his centre, his queen's knight is deprived of the c6-square. It can go to d7 or even a6, but it is seldom as effective there as on its natural c6-square.

Secondly, the bishop on c8 is horrified to find the centre cluttered with pawns on light squares. The doom mongers like to tell us that this bishop will never come to any good and will remain forever entombed inside a dungeon of black pawns. This is a massive exaggeration, as it can be activated by the manoeuvre ...Bd7-e8-h5, though there is no guarantee it will be particularly effective there; or it can be developed by ...b7-b6 and then ...Bb7 or even ...Ba6. On the whole the bishop prefers the latter approach, though it involves loosening the queenside pawns and making c6 into a potential target.

The third drawback is the famous hole on e5. In his rush to get a grip on the light squares, Black has left this dark square without any pawn cover. You might think 'so what?' since the light square blockade keeps the white dark-squared bishop, queen and rooks from getting anywhere near the e5-square.

But we mustn't forget the knights. Whereas every other piece has to stop when it encounters an obstacle along a file or diagonal, a knight can jump right through barriers. In Diagram 1, the white knight on f3 is already eyeing the e5-square with quiet satisfaction. Knights are short-range pieces and therefore love to be posted on centre squares where they can't be driven away by pawns. The e5-square fits the bill perfectly.

 NOTE: If White manages to station a knight permanently on e5, with no resistance from the black pieces, then everything else being equal, he will have an excellent game.

You won't see a book on the Stonewall that doesn't contain a position like one seen in Diagram 11.

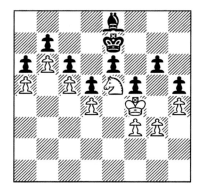

Diagram 11
Good knight versus terrible bishop!

Diagram 12 (W)
White needs a plan

Black has an extra pawn but that is all he has to be proud of. His bishop is a wretched piece and is tied down to e8, for if 1...Bf7 then 2 Nxc6! wins at once: 2...bxc6 3 b7 and the pawn queens. If it were White's move, he would win very easily by 1 Kg5 (not so much to capture on g6, but rather because it leaves Black in zugzwang) 1...Kf8 2 Kf6 Kg8 3 Ke7 and wins.

With Black to move, 1...Kf6 is harder to crack though 2 g4 does the trick: 2...hxg4 (or 2...Kg7 3 gxh5 gxh5 4 Kg5 Kh7 5 Kf6 etc.) 3 fxg4 Kg7 (3...fxg4 4 Kxg4 Kg7 5 Kg5 with zugzwang again – remember 5...Bf7 6 Nxc6!) 4 g5 Kf8 5 Nd3 (with the incidental threat of 6 Nb4 and 7 Nxa6!) 5...Bd7 6 Ke5 Ke7 7 Nf4 Be8 8 Nxe6 Bd7 9 Nf4 Be8 10 h5! gxh5 11 g6 h4 12 g7 Kf7 13 Kd6 Kxg7 14 Kc7 and White will queen his b-pawn long before Black can do anything with his passed pawns on the kingside.

Considering White's huge positional advantage (the pawn on b6 is a monster) it still took some precision to force the win. In most scenarios of this sort, the bishop is by no means as helpless as it is sometimes portrayed in books. There is usually a source of counterplay to be found somewhere, which allows the bishop to show its worth in the endgame as a long-range piece.

White's Strategy

Returning to the position after **1 d4 f5 2 g3 Nf6 3 Bg2 e6 4 Nf3 d5 5 c4 c6 6 0-0 Bd6 (Diagram 12)**, we can now put together a possible plan for White. There are three facets:

1) A queenside pawn advance: the c6-pawn already presents a target that can be rammed by b4-b5, and if Black plays ...b7-b6 to get the

light-squared bishop into the game then the c6-pawn is even more compromised.

2) Winning control of the e5-square for a white knight. This would be greatly facilitated if Black's dark-squared bishop were exchanged. There are two ways to offer an exchange of bishops: b2-b3 and then Ba3, or Bf4.

3) Ensuring as far as possible that Black's light-squared bishop has a miserable existence.

Bearing all these ideas in mind, let's see what happens when Black plays the same variation that brought him a 23-move win in the first game of the chapter, but this time against a steely opponent: top Australian grandmaster Ian Rogers.

Game 14
☐ I.Rogers ■ E.Montilla Carrillo
Cala Galdana 1999

1 d4 d5 2 Nf3 e6 3 g3 f5 4 Bg2 Nf6 5 0-0 Bd6 6 c4 c6 7 b3 Nbd7

Now Black is all geared up to start his attack but...

8 Ba3!

is a severe blow. Black is deprived of the services of his bishop, which played a leading role in the attack on h2.

8...Bxa3 9 Nxa3 0-0 (Diagram 13)

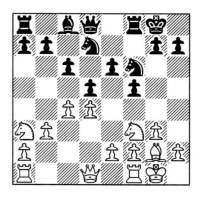

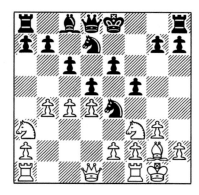

Diagram 13 (W)	Diagram 14 (B)
No kingside pawn storm	Undermining the queenside

Black renounces the kingside pawn storm. Indeed, not only is it lacking energy due to the absence of his king's bishop, but White is in a healthier state to meet it: the white bishop that stood like a statue on b2 in Game 11 is thankfully off the board, and the knight on a3 is somewhat surprisingly in a better state to help White generate counterplay than it would be on d2. There is an adage that a knight on the rim is dim, but when the centre is blocked that could well be the best place for it to be! Let's see what might have happened if Black had carried on attacking with 9...Ne4: 10 b4! **(Diagram 14)** and already White has active play based on undermining the pawn chain on c6 and d5.

There could follow 10...g5 11 b5 h5 (there is no way through after 11...g4 12 Nh4) 12 Rc1 h4 13 bxc6 bxc6 14 cxd5 cxd5 15 Nb5! threatening a very big fork on c7. If 15...Kf7 then 16 Rc6! looks tremendous.

Another try is 10...h5, but then 11 b5 h4 12 Nxh4 g5 13 Nf3 Qf6 14 Rc1 leaves Black with no way to exploit the h-file. For example, 14...f4 15 bxc6 (even simpler is 15 g4!) 15...bxc6 16 cxd5 exd5 17 Qc2 g4 18 Ne5 Qh6?! 19 Nxg4 etc.

Nonetheless, despite knowing that White holds all the positional aces after Black's wild kingside lunge, it is still frightening to be attacked in this fashion. It only needs the chess equivalent of one lucky bounce of the ball for the white king to end up being mated.

10 Nc2!

Over the next three moves the white knight heads single-mindedly towards d3, where it can see nirvana on e5.

10...Ne4

The e4-square isn't as hospitable as e5 is for a white knight, as the black knight faces being kicked away by a future f2-f3.

11 Nce1 Ndf6?

Black should have seized the moment for 11...f4 when after 12 Nd3 fxg3 13 hxg3 he has the f-file and it is harder for White to arrange to evict the knight with a future f2-f3 as it would leave the g3-pawn hanging.

WARNING: You have to take your chances for activity as Black in the Dutch. Routine developing moves can land you into hot water.

12 Nd3 (Diagram 15)

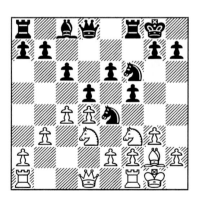

Diagram 15 (B)
Eyeing e5

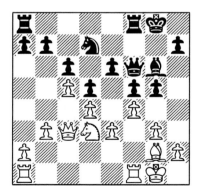

Diagram 16 (B)
Blocking the kingside

Now White takes control.

12...Bd7 13 Nfe5!

White had little difficulty in choosing which knight to honour with the post on e5. The knight on f3 has few other options, whereas the knight on d3 plays a role on both sides of the board: it helps suppress ...f5-f4 ideas by Black on the kingside, and both supports b2-b4 and observes the c5-square on the queenside. Another important consideration is that White wants to clear the way for f2-f3.

13...Be8 14 e3

A useful precaution as Black threatened 14...dxc4, uncovering an attack on d4.

14...Nd7

Here 14...g5 15 f3 Nd6, intending ...Bh5, might have been the best hope for counterplay.

15 f3 Nxe5 16 Nxe5 Nf6 17 Qc2 Nd7 18 Nd3!

Generally speaking, the exchange of a pair of minor pieces earlier in the game has favoured White as it takes the dynamism out of a black counterattack on the kingside. But here White rightly declines more exchanges as the black knight has less scope than the white knight on d3. The black bishop is also left cluttering up the back rank.

TIP: If you have more space, keep pieces on the board; if you have less, exchange off pieces.

It may seem that Black has done well to evict the white knight from e5, but remember it has been at the cost of neglecting an aggressive plan of attack on the kingside. White, meanwhile, is all prepared for a queenside pawn advance.

18...Qf6 19 Qc3 g5

At last the familiar pawn advance, but the forces to support it are sadly diminished compared to the Harzer and Botvinnik games above.

20 c5 Bg6 21 f4! (Diagram 16)

An essential precaution: Black isn't even allowed to dream about a breakout such as 21 b4?? f4! 22 exf4 Bxd3 23 Qxd3 gxf4, when suddenly Black is rid of his bad bishop and has a strong kingside initiative. Just one careless move can ruin an excellent strategical build-up.

WARNING: In the Dutch you have to be on the constant lookout for tactical breakthroughs, both for you and the opponent.

21...g4

The immediate 21...h5 looks a more fighting move. Now White has only to make sure no disaster strikes him down the h-file before his queenside build-up becomes overpowering.

22 b4 Rfc8 23 a4 Be8

Black's last two moves make a pitiful contrast to the attacking panache he displayed in the games above.

24 Rfc1 a6 25 Bf1 h5 26 Ra3 Qh6 27 b5 h4

Both sides advance pawns on the same move, but White's breakthrough along the b-file is much more telling than Black's on the kingside. In fact, Black's advance is so badly supported by the pieces other than the queen that he soon loses control of the h-file.

28 bxc6 bxc6 29 Rb3 hxg3 30 hxg3 Ra7 31 Rc2! (Diagram 17)

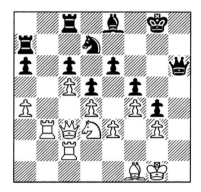 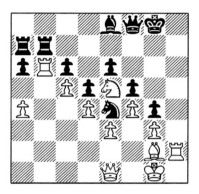

| Diagram 17 (B) | Diagram 18 (B) |
| Preparing Rh2 | White infiltrates |

Just in time to stop Black getting any counterplay with 31...Rh7, though Rogers would have made sure his rook arrived on h2 before the black rook on h7 even if Black had been any faster.

31...Nf6 32 Rh2 Qf8 33 Ne5

So the white knight gets to return to e5. Positionally speaking, White is now completely winning as he has the open b-file and a fixed target on c6 – and, vitally, Black has not the slightest counterplay. The black bishop on e8 in particular is a dreadful piece.

33...Ne4 34 Qe1 Rcc7 35 Bg2 Rcb7 36 Rb6! (Diagram 18)

An important move. Black can only get rid of the rook at the cost of allowing a passed pawn after 36...Rxb6 37 cxb6. If he just waits then 37 Bxe4 followed by 38 Qb4 would gradually push him off the board. Black therefore makes a desperate sacrifice that is convincingly refuted.

36...Nxc5 37 Qb4! Rxb6 38 Qxb6 Rb7 39 Qxc5 Qxc5 40 dxc5 Rb1+ 41 Bf1 Rc1 42 Rh6 Bf7 43 Rf6 1-0

An excellent game that demonstrated the three central themes of White's strategy in the Stonewall: winning control of e5, staging a queenside breakthrough and exploiting the bad black bishop.

Such is the high level of chess played these days that this strategic masterpiece was played in Division 2 of the Spanish League.

Meeting White's pressure by remoulding or dissolving the Pawn Centre

In the unsophisticated examples at the beginning of the chapter, Black regarded his centre as forever fixed on the spot, and went off hunting with his pieces with moves like ...Ne4, ...Qe8 and ...Qh5, ...g7-g5 etc. Nothing wrong with that: as we saw this sort of crude attacking strategy can work out very well, especially if you are a future world champion like Botvinnik.

However, as you climb the ladder towards your own world title you will discover that White is less and less willing to let you walk all over him. You'll start to find that your pawn centre isn't quite as indestructible as you imagined, and for some reason things will occasionally go very wrong on the queenside.

When you reach the level at which this is happening frequently enough to shake your faith in the Stonewall, it is time to forgo the direct plan of attack in favour of more advanced positional methods.

Remember that in an earthquake, buildings are designed to sway with the tremors. If they tried to resist the vibrations they would be shattered. In the same way, Black mustn't always meet White's attempt to exert pressure on the centre in a purely static manner: he must be prepared to react flexibly – this may involve voluntarily dismantling his centre with a move like ...d5xc4 or ...d5xe4 followed by ...c6-c5 or ...e6-e5.

TIP: If you are playing Black and your centre is about to vanish, make sure it happens on your own terms rather than your opponent's.

Black's light-squared Bishop Reappraised

In an endgame Black's light-squared bishop can be a poor piece. Still, as Tartakower remarked, before the endgame the gods have placed the middlegame, and here the bishop can be an excellent piece. Sometimes this is because it manages to escape outside the pawn structure to h5, where it joins in a kingside attack; but more often than not it is content to lurk patiently in the background, say on b7, waiting for the black pawn structure in the centre to dissolve. Many times White has rejoiced at destroying the stonewall centre, only to find that he is then struck down by the dynamic black pieces, with the light-squared bishop at the forefront of the counterattack!

In case you need convincing, in the following example the bishop has the honour of delivering checkmate.

Game 15
☐ H.Olafsson ■ S.Agdestein
Reykjavik 1987

1 d4 e6 2 c4 f5 3 g3 Nf6 4 Bg2 c6 (Diagram 19)

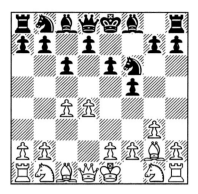
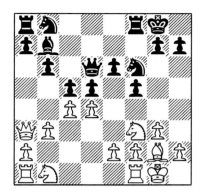

| **Diagram 19 (W)** | **Diagram 20 (W)** |
| A flexible move order | 12...c6-c5! |

Black's move order deserves to be remarked upon, as Simen Agdestein has long been one of the world's leading Stonewall experts. The idea of delaying ...d7-d5 is so that 5 Nh3 can be answered with 5...d6 when Black has maintained the flexibility to drive away the white knight after 6 Nf4? with 6...e5 (alternatively Black can first play 5...Bb4+, getting the bishop out of the pawn chain, and only then ...d7-d6). Though having said that, top Stonewall players like Short and Bareev have answered 5 Nh3 with 5...d5, so perhaps it is all a bluff!

5 Nf3 d5 6 0-0 Bd6 7 b3 Qe7!

This is an important part of Black's set-up and much better than 7...Nbd7 in the Rogers game above. White is prevented from playing his favourite move 8 Ba3.

8 Bb2 b6

And here Black shows regard for his light-squared bishop, which in the previous game ended up in a wasteland on e8. Agdestein intends to show that, if handled correctly, it can be Black's most powerful piece.

9 Qc1 0-0 10 Ba3

White has had to expend two more moves' worth of energy (Bb2 and Qc1) than in the Rogers game to force the strategically desirable exchange of bishops.

10...Bb7 11 Bxd6 Qxd6 12 Qa3 c5! (Diagram 20)

After the exchange of queens with 12...Qxa3 13 Nxa3, White could settle down to the long-term business of putting pressure on the queenside with b3-b4 etc. Black would be a long way from losing, but it wouldn't be much fun and his winning chances would be remote. Therefore, Agdestein transforms the pawn centre so that he has so-called hanging pawns. He hopes that the white queen will prove to be shut out of the game on a3 whilst he can attack on the kingside. Of course, it all depends on the black centre holding firm under White's heavy pressure.

13 dxc5 bxc5 14 Nc3 Nbd7 15 Rfd1 f4! (Diagram 21)

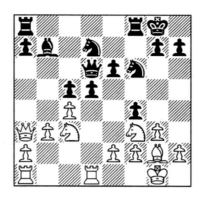 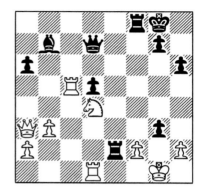

Diagram 21 (W)
Striving for the initiative

Diagram 22 (W)
24...fxg3!!

If instead 15...d4? then 16 Rxd4 wins a pawn. Therefore Agdestein stakes everything on kingside counterplay.

16 Rac1 a6 17 Bh3

Black's centre is being probed from all directions by the white pieces, which are searching for a way to demolish it.

17...Rae8 18 Rc2 h6

Every black unit is being pressed into service. The rook's pawns are now restraining White from playing Nb5 on the queenside and Ng5 on the kingside.

19 Na4?

Overconfidence often leads to miscalculation. White should have settled for a safe move such as 19 Rcd2 with unclear play.

19...Ne4! 20 cxd5 exd5 21 Bxd7 Qxd7 22 Nxc5 Nxc5 23 Rxc5

Not 23 Qxc5? Rec8, winning a rook. White achieves his aim of conquering c5 but now e2 drops, leading to an unexpected disaster on the kingside.

23...Rxe2 24 Nd4

It looks as though White has a huge positional advantage: after all, the beautiful knight on d4 is shutting in a bad bishop on b7. But Black's next move turns the position on its head.

24...fxg3!! (Diagram 22)

The move White had missed. If now 25 Nxe2 then 25...gxf2+ 26 Kg2 Qg4+ 27 Ng3 d4+ 28 Kf1 Qxd1 is mate.

25 fxg3 Qf7!

Now White has no choice but to take the rook, after which the much-maligned 'bad' bishop has the last laugh.

26 Nxe2 Qf2+ 27 Kh1 d4+ 28 Rd5 Bxd5 mate (0-1)

Game 16
□ **V.Sergeev** ■ **I.Glek**
Vladimir 2004

Here the Stonewall occurred via a Classical move order.

1 d4 e6 2 c4 f5 3 g3 Nf6 4 Bg2 Bb4+ 5 Bd2 Bxd2+ 6 Qxd2 0-0 7 Nc3 d5 8 Nf3 c6 9 0-0 Nbd7!?

More usual is 9...Ne4 10 Qc2. By delaying ...Ne4, Glek gives his opponent the chance to go wrong.

TIP: A new or little-known opening move is seldom objectively stronger than the established moves: its power is in confronting the opponent with a set of unfamiliar problems.

10 Qe3

White puts his queen on a square where she proves to be vulnerable. The proper reply appears to be 10 Qc2, without waiting to be 'asked' by ...Ne4. Then 10...dxc4 11 e4 gives White the initiative, while 10...Ne4 11 b4 allows him to build up on the queenside with some advantage.

10...Re8 11 b3 (Diagram 23)

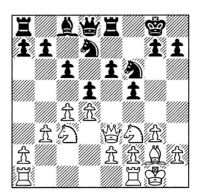

Diagram 23 (B)
Time for a change of structure

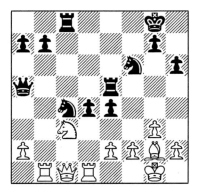

Diagram 24 (W)
...d5-d4: a tactical trick

Perhaps White intended 11 Ne5, but then 11...Nxe5 12 Qxe5 Qb6!? 13 b3 Ng4! 14 Qf4 dxc4 15 bxc4 e5 breaks out with the advantage.

11...dxc4!

GM Igor Glek is possibly the world's leading expert on the Stonewall, but here he ruthlessly demolishes it in order to transform the pawn structure into one favourable to him.

12 bxc4 e5 13 d5?

Psychologically it is always difficult for White to admit he has lost his opening advantage. Here the submissive 13 dxe5 was necessary, when 13...Ng4 14 Qf4 Ndxe5 15 Rfd1 is only slightly worse for White: it is easier to defend one weak pawn than two.

13...e4 14 Nd4 Ne5!

Now 15 dxc6 Nxc4 wins the knight on d4, so White is going to drop a centre pawn.

15 Qg5 h6 16 Qf4 Nxc4 17 Nxf5 Bxf5 18 Qxf5 cxd5 19 Rfd1 Re5 20 Qf4 Qa5 21 Qc1 Rc8 22 Rb1 d4! (Diagram 24)

A piece of tactical flashiness livens up the dour exploitation of the pawn advantage. Black clears the d5-square in order to pin and win the knight on c3.

23 Rxd4 Nb6!

An admirable manoeuvre as it is well known that retreating moves by well-placed knights are difficult to foresee.

24 Rb3 Nbd5 25 Qb2 Nxc3 26 Bh3 Rc7 27 Kg2 Kh7 28 a4 Qc5 29 Rd8 Nxa4 30 Qa1 Nc3 0-1

Meeting White's pressure by controlling Key Squares

The above games demonstrated the value of modifying or even dismantling the Stonewall pawn structure in order to escape long-term pressure. Next I want to look at a couple of examples in which Black held firm in the centre but frustrated White's plan of a queenside advance by creating impenetrable strong points on the light squares.

Game 17
□ **C.Gokhale** ■ **K.Spraggett**
Kapuskasing 2004

1 d4 f5 2 g3 Nf6 3 Bg2 e6 4 c4 Be7 5 Nf3 0-0 6 0-0 Ne4 7 Qc2 Bf6 8 Nc3 d5 9 Ne5 c6 10 f3 Nd6 11 c5 Nf7 12 f4 Nxe5 13 fxe5 Be7 (Diagram 25)

White would like to play an immediate 14 b4 to start a queenside expansion, but Black can then counterattack with 14...a5 15 b5 (of course 15 a3 is the tidy move but it fails to 15...axb4, exploiting the pin along the a-file) 15...b6!, when the advanced white pawns are liquidated, relieving all the pressure on Black's queenside. So Gokhale played

14 Bd2

The idea is to follow up with 15 b4 and answer 15...a5 with 16 a3, thereby keeping the spearhead on c5 firmly supported. In reply Spraggett bolstered the b5-square against any White advance.

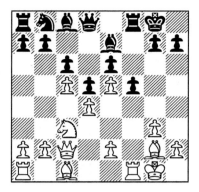

Diagram 25 (W)
How should White proceed?

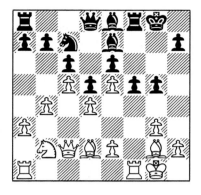

Diagram 26 (W)
Getting on with it

14...Na6! 15 a3 Nc7 16 b4 Bd7

Now White has no constructive plan: he can never punch through the b-file with a pawn as Black can cover the b5-square again with ...a7-a6 when necessary. A player without the guiding light of a plan is doomed to waiting to see what his opponent comes up with, which is bad news at the best of times but especially when you are playing a grandmaster.

17 Nd1 Be8 18 Nb2 g5! (Diagram 26)

In contrast to his opponent's strategical inertia, Black has a clear plan of gaining space on the kingside and then starting a direct attack on the white king. The ...g7-g5 advance entails no risk whatsoever to the black king as White's pieces are unable to get anywhere close to him.

19 Nd3 Bg6 20 a4 a6

Ending once and for all any white activity on the queenside.

21 Qc1 Kh8 22 Rf2 Rg8 23 Ne1 Bh5 24 Nf3 Rg7

Black begins to clear the way for his rook on a8 to enter the fray on the kingside. He is in no hurry to force matters: psychologically this is an astute approach, as it gives White the chance to become frustrated and weaken himself, as occurs in the game.

25 Ra3 h6 26 Ne1 Qd7 27 Bf3 Bf7 28 h3 Rag8 29 Rh2 Rh7 30 Bg2 Bd8 31 Kf2 Be8 32 Nf3 Bh5 33 h4? (Diagram 27)

White loses patience and tries to attack on the kingside, but the black pieces and pawns are much better deployed to take advantage of the open lines. White should have kept everything as solid as possible and awaited Black's assault, but it is far easier to give advice like this than to take it!

33...Qg7 34 hxg5 hxg5 35 Qh1 Qg6 36 Ne1 Rgg7 37 Bf3 Bg4 38 Ra1 Rxh2+ 39 Qxh2+ Rh7 40 Qg2 Bh3 41 Qg1 Rh6 42 Bh1 f4!

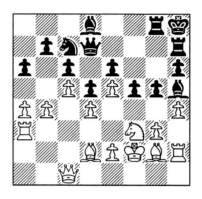

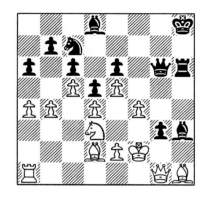

Diagram 27 (B)
Losing patience

Diagram 28 (W)
It's all over

At last it is the right moment to stage a pawn breakthrough.

43 gxf4 g4 44 Nd3 g3+ 0-1 (Diagram 28)

For if 45 Qxg3 then 45...Bh4. A fine strategic performance by Black.

Game 18
□ **B.Lalic** ■ **K.Spraggett**
Zaragoza 1996

1 d4 f5 2 Nf3 Nf6 3 g3 e6 4 Bg2 Be7 5 c4 0-0 6 0-0 Ne4 7 Qc2 Bf6 8 Nc3 d5 9 Bf4 c6 10 Rab1 Nd7 11 Rfd1 g5 12 Bc1 Qe7 13 b4 a6 14 Ne1 (Diagram 29)

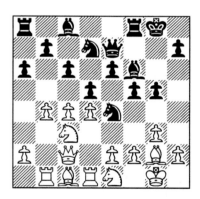

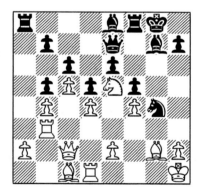

Diagram 29 (B)
Black takes action

Diagram 30 (W)
22...Nf6-g4!

Here Black took action to relieve the pressure on his queenside.

14...Nd6! 15 c5 Nb5!

If instead 15...Nc4? then White has the chance to expand in the centre with 16 e4!, as 16...fxe4?! 17 Nxe4 dxe4? 18 Qxc4 leaves Black with splintered pawns.

16 Nxb5

The d4-pawn was hanging, and if 16 e3 then 16...Nxc3 17 Qxc3 e5 is very active for Black.

16...axb5

Black can be very pleased with the results of his play on the queenside. He has the a4-square firmly in his grasp, as it is difficult to see how White can ever get his knight to c3 to support a2-a4. Therefore, White lacks a queenside pawn storm, though his pieces have more space to counter the kingside pressure here than in the Gokhale game above.

17 f4!

White makes the best of a bad situation. Here he prevents Black from gaining space in the centre with 17...e5.

17...gxf4 18 gxf4 Bg7!

Clearing the way for the knight to get to f6, which in turn clears the way for the bishop on c8 to get to d7.

19 Nf3 Nf6 20 Ne5 Bd7 21 Kh1 Be8 22 Rb3!

White defends very well, which is just what you would expect from GM Bogdan Lalic.

22...Ng4! (Diagram 30)

Note that the natural 22...Ne4? is a bad mistake as the white rooks can swing to the kingside after 23 Bxe4 dxe4 24 Rg3 and then 25 Rdg1 when suddenly White has a fierce attack.

23 Rf1 Qh4 24 Nf3 Qh5 25 h3 Kh8 26 Kg1 Nf6 27 Ne5 Ne4 28 Kh2 Bxe5 29 fxe5 Rg8

and Black had the initiative on the kingside, though White managed to hold the draw with a spirited defence.

30 Bf4 Bf7 31 Bxe4 dxe4 32 Rg3 Rxg3 33 Kxg3 Rg8+ 34 Kh2 Qh4 35 e3 Bh5 36 Qf2 Qxf2+ 37 Rxf2 Bf3 38 a3 h5 39 Bg3 Kg7 40 Ra2 Kf7 41 h4 Ke7 42 a4 Ra8 ½-½

White Plays Bf4

So far the emphasis has been on White playing b2-b3 and then Ba3. However, there is another method of offering the strategically desirable exchange of dark-squared bishops – the direct Bf4. For example:

1 d4 f5 2 c4 Nf6 3 g3 e6 4 Bg2 c6 5 Nf3 d5 6 0-0 Bd6 7 Bf4 (Diagram 31) Bxf4 8 gxf4 (Diagram 32)

Who has benefited most from the change in pawn structure? After ...Bd6xf4 and the recapture g3xf4, White has an impressive-looking grip over the e5-square, which makes it hard to see how Black could ever hope to free his game with ...e6-e5. On the other hand, the white kingside pawn structure has lost its flexibility – if White ever tries to advance e2-e4 himself it is going to fall to pieces. Furthermore, a pawn structure that is set in stone can never adjust itself to take account of pressure exerted upon it. Therefore, Black has a clear plan for counterattack: the preparation of ...g7-g5 to undermine the f4-pawn and break open the g-file for the rooks.

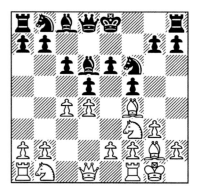

Diagram 31 (B)
White offers an exchange

Diagram 32 (B)
Who has benefited most?

In this set-up the black bishop on c8 often finds itself well placed on h5, as there is little to harass it there (White no longer has the option of Nh3 and Nf4) and also because it can aid the advance ...g7-g5 by putting pressure on the white knight on f3.

Game 19
☐ **G.Hernandez Himenez** ■ **V.Moskalenko**
Barcelona 2001

1 d4 f5 2 c4 Nf6 3 g3 e6 4 Bg2 c6 5 Nf3 d5 6 0-0 Bd6 7 Bf4 Bxf4 8 gxf4 h6!? (Diagram 3)

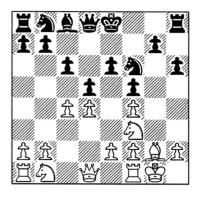

Diagram 33 (W)
No positional niceties

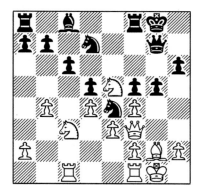

Diagram 34 (W)
Threatening ...Nd2

A throwback to the first game in the chapter. Black doesn't let any positional niceties like development get in the way of his preparation for a kingside attack.

9 e3 Qc7

This move has the positional justification of getting the queen to the g-file as fast as possible. It isn't just to set up a cheap trap against h2, though that also comes in handy!

10 Nc3 g5

Strategy justified by tactics: 11 fxg5 hxg5 12 Nxg5 Qxh2 mate.

11 Ne5 Qg7 12 Rc1 Nbd7 13 Qf3

A rather nervous move. The queen proves misplaced here, so White should have gone about bolstering the defences along the g-file with 13 Kh1 and 14 Rg1, when the position is sharply balanced.

13...0-0 14 cxd5 exd5 15 b4 Ne4 (Diagram 34)

Here we see the drawback to White's 13th move: if the queen were still on d1 he could press ahead with 16 b5 here, but now this loses the exchange to 16...Nd2. Therefore White has to lose a move with his queen.

16 Qe2 Kh7 17 Kh1 Nxe5 18 dxe5?

A serious mistake. After 18 fxe5! Nxc3 19 Rxc3 f4 20 b5! a full scale battle would be raging between White's queenside pressure and Black's kingside counterplay – a typical Dutch scenario in fact, in which the best man or woman would come out on top as either colour.

18...gxf4 19 exf4 Qe7 20 Qh5 Be6 21 Bh3 Qe8!

Black is no longer interested in a middlegame tussle on the wings as in the endgame he has a definite positional advantage in the centre. White should avoid the exchange of queens but he goes meekly to his doom.

22 Qxe8? Raxe8 (Diagram 35)

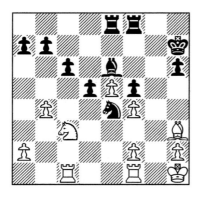

Diagram 35 (W)
An endgame advantage

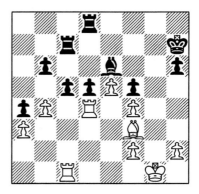

Diagram 36 (W)
The queenside pawns are rolling

So what exactly is the nature of Black's advantage? The fact is the protected passed pawn on e5 may look impressive, but it is going nowhere: White's four pawns on the kingside are comfortably held by Black's two pawns. In contrast, Black has a 4-2 majority of pawns on the queenside, and there is nothing to stop them rolling forwards.

23 Ne2 a5! 24 a3 Nd2 25 Rfd1 Nb3 26 Rc3 a4 27 Nd4 Nxd4 28 Rxd4 Rc8 29 Bf1 Rg8 30 Be2 b6 31 Rc1 Rg7 32 Ba6 Rcg8 33 Be2

Of course 33 Rxc6 allows mate in one – the g-file proves useful after all.

33...Rc7 34 Bf3 Rd8 35 Kg1 c5! (Diagram 36)

Black can afford to give up the a4-pawn as the connected passed pawns in the centre will be overwhelming.

36 bxc5 bxc5 37 Rxa4 d4 38 Kf1 d3 39 Kg1 d2 40 Rd1 c4 41 Ra6 c3 0-1

White Plays Nh3

As we saw in the above section, the plan of Bf4 misses its mark somewhat as the pawn structure that results after the exchange ...Bxf4, g3xf4 gives Black definite chances of counterplay. A more subtle version of this plan would be to play Nh3 and only then Bf4, when if Black exchanges on f4 White can recapture with Nxf4. In this way White avoids the dislocation of his pawn structure and brings his knight to a powerful centre square.

We should make it clear that the plan of Nh3 and Nf4 is also interesting even if not associated with the Bf4 idea. This is especially the case if Black has entered the Stonewall set up via a Classical move order, in which he has played ...Be7 rather than ...Bd6: in that case Nh3 and Nf4 is attractive, as there is no bishop on d6 to lop off the knight and force the recapture g3xf4.

Game 20
☐ **V.Anand** ■ **Pr.Nikolic**
Wijk aan Zee 2000

---

1 d4 f5 2 g3 Nf6 3 Bg2 e6 4 c4 d5 5 Nh3

As we saw in Game 15, if Black is averse to facing the Nh3 move in the Stonewall he can employ a sequence of opening moves designed to evade it: 1 d4 e6 2 c4 f5 3 g3 Nf6 4 Bg2 c6 5 Nh3 d6!? (or 5 Nf3 d5).

5...c6 6 0-0 Bd6 7 Qc2 0-0 8 Nd2

After 8 Bf4 an interesting reply is 8...Be7!? declining the exchange of bishops. Then the white knight is left looking dismal on h3 and the bishop on f4 can be targeted with ...h7-h6 and ...g7-g5, thereby gaining time for Black's kingside counterplay.

8...Bd7? (Diagram 37)

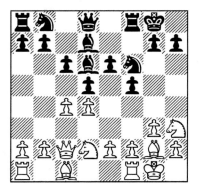

Diagram 37 (W)
8...Bd7 – not the best

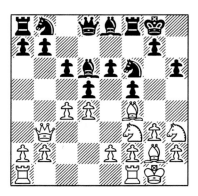

Diagram 38 (B)
Provoking a weakness

A better try was 8...h6!, which threatens to cut off the knight on h3 immediately with ...g7-g5. After 9 Nf4 (9 Nf3 g5!) 9...Bxf4 10 gxf4 we have the pawn structure familiar to us from the Bf4 section above. With the centre blocked, the fact that Black has given up the bishop for the white knight, rather than the white bishop, could actually be to his advantage. It certainly turned out that way in the following example: 10...Bd7 11 b3 Kh8 12 Nf3 Be8 13 Ne5 Nbd7 14 Kh1 Bh5 15 b4 dxc4! (this is a classic instance of knowing when to disband the pawn centre in return for activating the pieces, as the black knight will be a star on d5) 16 Qxc4 Nd5 17 Rb1 Nxe5 18 dxe5 Qh4 19 Rb3 b5! 20 Qxc6 Bxe2 21 Rg1 Nxf4 and White's position crumbled in Babula-Nikolic, Panormo 2001.

You will notice that both the main game and this extract were played by Bosnian GM Predrag Nikolic. The Anand game was in the year 2000; the Babula game in 2001. Therefore Nikolic must have studied his game with Anand, perhaps even in a post mortem with the Indian world champion himself, and deduced that he should have obstructed White's kingside build up with the immediate 8...h6!. He then got the chance to test the improvement versus Babula in the later game. That is the way theory advances: the world champions like Anand are at the forefront in discovering new ideas, closely followed by top GMs like Nikolic, and finally their ideas filter down to the rest of us in books!

9 Nf3

Now White has the opportunity to offer the exchange of bishops on f4 and recapture with the knight on h3.

9...Be8 10 Bf4 h6 11 Qb3! (Diagram 38)

Anand provokes a weakness in Black's queenside on c6 before putting a rook on c1.

11...b6

Normally Black only wants to play this move if he intends to put his bishop on b7. However, it was hard to see how it could be avoided without causing Black trouble with his development.

12 Rfc1 Be7

An idea discussed at move eight above, but it turns out badly as White has too much pressure on the queenside. Still, it is hard to suggest anything else, as 12...Bxf4 Nxf4 is equally unpleasant for Black.

13 cxd5! Nxd5

After 13...cxd5 14 Bc7! Qd7 15 Ne5 Qb5 16 Nf4 Black's defences are falling apart, while 13...exd5 14 Ne5 leaves Black tied to the c6-pawn without even a well-placed knight on d5.

14 Bd2 g5 (Diagram 39)

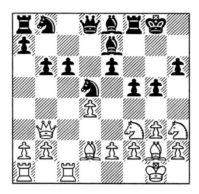

Diagram 39 (W)	Diagram 40 (B)
Preventing Nf4	Playing without a knight

The attempt to keep the white knight out of f4 is understandable, but after White's next move there is no way to develop the knight on b8 without dropping c6. Therefore Anand is able to launch a direct attack on the black king to exploit his more active pieces, and the loosening of Black's kingside proves very handy.

15 Ne5 a5 16 e4! fe4 17 Bxe4 Ra7 18 f4 gxf4 19 Kh1!

White avoids any tricks based on ...Qxd4+ and clears the g-file for his major pieces.

19...Bf6 20 Nxf4 Qd6 21 Nfg6 Bxg6 22 Nxg6 Rff7 23 Bf4!

This gets rid of Black's best-placed minor piece: the knight on d5.

23...Nxf4 24 gxf4 Bg7 25 Qh3 (Diagram 40)

If you want a simple reason why White now has a winning attack, you need look no further than the fact that Black spends the whole game with his knight sitting on b8. You can't give Anand piece odds!

25...Rf6 26 Rc3 Qxd4 27 Qg2 Rd7 28 Rg1 b5 29 Rg3 Qa7 30 Ne5 Re7 31 Qd2 Qc7 32 Rd3 Re8 33 Rd6 c5 34 Ng4 Rff8 35 Nxh6+

Kh8 36 Ng4 Rd8 37 Qg2 Rxd6 38 Qh3+ Kg8 39 Qh7+ Kf7 40 Bg6+
1-0

White Avoids g3

It is relatively rare for White to avoid Bg2 against the Stonewall.
Usually it comes about 'by accident' when after 1 d4 d5 2 c4 c6 3 Nc3
e6 4 e3 (the Meran Variation of the Slav), Black suddenly plays 4...f5
and we have a Stonewall.

Game 21
□ **B.Gelfand** ■ **N.Short**
Tilburg 1990

---

1 d4 e6 2 c4 f5 3 Nc3 Nf6 4 e3 d5

A Classical treatment with 4...Bb4!? might well be the best response
to White's set-up.

5 Bd3 c6 6 h3!?

A very ambitious idea. Instead after 6 Nf3 Bd6 7 0-0 0-0 followed by
...Bd7 and ...Be8, with ...a7-a5 and ...Qe7 thrown in if White threatened to gain space with b2-b4, Black would have reasonable chances.

6...Bd6 7 g4 (Diagram 41)

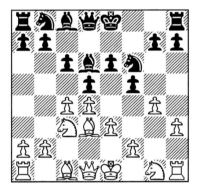
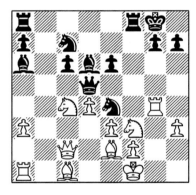

Diagram 41 (W)	**Diagram 42 (B)**
A simple plan	A combination looms...

White's plan is simple: break open the g-file, castle queenside and
then deliver mate on g7. If this strategy worked then it would be the
end of the road for the Stonewall. Fortunately, Nigel Short is on top
form and counterattacks energetically.

7...0-0 8 Qc2 Na6!

The annoying threat of 9...Nb4 not only forces White to lose time with
his next move, but also creates a target on a3 which Short exploits to
the maximum.

9 a3 dxc4! 10 Bxc4 b5 11 Be2 b4! 12 Na4

Now there can be no question of a straightforward attack by White down the g-file. The queenside is no longer a safe place for his king and his pieces have lost their coordination.

12...bxa3 13 bxa3 Ne4

You will be familiar by now with the strength of the black knight on e4 when it is unopposed.

14 Nf3 Qa5+ 15 Kf1 Nc7 16 Nb2 Ba6 17 Nc4 Qd5 18 Rg1 fxg4 19 Rxg4 (Diagram 42)

At last White has got his rook onto the open g-file, but it only gets to enjoy it for one move.

19...Ng3+! 20 Rxg3

Alas, if 20 fxg3 then 20...Rxf3+ 21 Bxf3 Qxf3+ 22 Kg1 Rf8 leaves White about to be poleaxed either along the f-file or with 23...Bxg3. The game move fights on, but there is no hope the exchange down against a former world title challenger.

20...Bxg3 21 Kg2

Or 21 fxg3 Rxf3+ as in the last note, but even worse for White.

21...Bh4 22 e4 Qh5 23 Nxh4 Qxh4 24 Be3 Rf6 25 Rh1 Raf8 26 Rh2 Rxf2+ 27 Bxf2 Qxf2+ 28 Kh1 Qe1+ 0-1

Chapter Five

Classical Dutch: Introduction And Main Line

Introduction

1 d4 f5 2 g3 Nf6 3 Bg2 e6 4 Nf3 Be7 5 0-0 0-0 6 c4 d6 **(Diagram 1)**

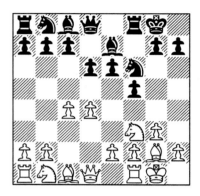

Diagram 1 (W)	**Diagram 2 (W)**
The Classical Dutch	A viable move order

Diagram 1 is the starting position for the Classical Dutch main line. It is characterised by the moves 3...e6, creating a post for the bishop on e7, and 6...d6, forming a mini-centre and guarding the e5-square. In contrast, the Leningrad puts the bishop on g7 while the Stonewall counters White's space advantage with ...d7-d5.

The Classical Dutch is well named because the no-nonsense development of the bishop on e7 has a 'classical' feel about it, in direct contrast to the 'modern' deployment of the bishop on g7. It has also appeared in some great classical games of the past featuring Alekhine and others. And, above all, it was used by Paul Morphy back in the 1850s (though not so many times: overall, Morphy had the Dutch Defence five times, and the Queen's Gambit three times as Black; the world's greatest player only faced 1 d4 eight times in his adult playing career!).

It is also know as the Dutch Fluid Centre, which sums up its flexibility, or the Ilyin-Genevsky System. Alexander Ilyin was a strong Soviet player and Dutch devotee. He won the championship of Geneva in 1914 and was evidently so pleased that thereafter he appended the name of the city to his own. He was Leningrad Champion three times and died there during the siege in 1941.

A Note on Move Order

The Dutch move order with 1 d4 f5 is given above, but remember that there are definite practical advantages in playing 1...e6!? **(Diagram 2)** first, and reaching the Classical Dutch via a move order such as 2 c4 f5. This is the method most strong players prefer nowadays, and was also the choice of Botvinnik. It cuts out having to learn what to do against the Staunton Gambit and the other lines in Chapter 1, while if White plays 2 Bg5?? as in Chapter 2, well, you can just take it! The possible drawback is that after 1...e6 White can play 2 e4, when suddenly you are in a French Defence. It probably won't happen, as most 1 d4 players shy away from transposing to a king's pawn opening, but you have to be ready for it.

The Pros and Cons of the Classical Dutch

If we wish to be critical of the way Black has set out his game in Diagram 1, then two obvious objections spring to mind. Firstly, unlike in the Stonewall, he has made no immediate challenge to White's space advantage in the centre with ...d7-d5. And secondly, the bishop on e7 is far worse off than in the Stonewall where it commands two diagonals on d6, or in the Leningrad where from g7 it puts pressure on the d4-square. In fact, the bishop on e7 literally can't do anything – it is stalemated!

So much for the bad features of Black's position; now for the good news. In contrast to the Stonewall, here he has kept the e5-square under guard, so there is no gaping wound in the centre of his pawn chain. If Black does eventually play ...d7-d5, then it could be regarded as a Stonewall in slow motion; but this doesn't necessarily mean that Black has just lost time. On the contrary, by keeping White guessing about his plans he forces his opponent to commit his pieces to squares which aren't their optimum development versus the Stonewall. For example, Black could wait until White played b2-b3 and Bb2 before playing ...d6-d5, which sidesteps ideas of Bf4 or an immediate Ba3.

Naturally Black has many other options besides the preparation of ...d6-d5. Under favourable circumstances it might be possible to play ...e6-e5, freeing his bishop on c8 and creating a dynamic pawn centre. Alternatively, he might decide to keep the status quo in the centre and try for kingside pressure with the manoeuvre ...Qe8 and then ...Qg6 or in some cases ...Qh5.

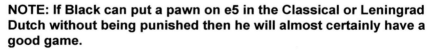

NOTE: If Black can put a pawn on e5 in the Classical or Leningrad Dutch without being punished then he will almost certainly have a good game.

It can also prove useful that, in contrast to the Leningrad, Black has avoided weakening his kingside pawn structure with ...g7-g6. He can put his bishop all the same on its favourite diagonal with the typical sequence ...Ne4 followed by ...Bf6. The knight is usually a marvellous piece on e4, right in the thick of the action; and if White ever exchanges it off with Nxe4 then, after the recapture ...f5xe4, Black's e4-pawn can be readily supported by ...d6-d5. This isn't usually the case in the Leningrad, where Black has played ...d7-d6 rather than ...e7-e6.

Finally, here is one of the best arguments in favour of the Classical over the Stonewall: because Black has delayed committing himself with ...d7-d5, he has pretty much neutralised White's side variations involving the development Nh3 rather than the usual Nf3. This will be fully examined along with other divergences from the main line in the next chapter.

Therefore, we can conclude that in the Classical many of the positive ideas of the Leningrad and Stonewall are still available for Black, whilst some of the evils of these systems have been avoided. It is a beautifully flexible opening.

Theoretical?

Much less so than the Leningrad, a little bit more so than the Stonewall. There is still plenty of scope for imagination and creative thinking here – the two things that theory tends to discourage.

Black Opposes e2-e4 with ...Qg6

Starting from Diagram 1, the natural plan for White is to prepare the pawn advance e2-e4. The obvious sequence of moves to implement this is 7 Nc3, 8 Re1 and then 9 e4. This would virtually force the removal by exchange of the f5-pawn, as White can't be allowed to seize even more space in the centre with e4-e5. Therefore, besides reclaiming the e4-square, the pawn advance e2-e4 would open up a line of attack against the backward pawn on e6.

All this is of course easier said than done. Black has many resources, which range from trying to prevent e2-e4 altogether to allowing the advance and then exploiting some tactical motifs. First, let's consider what happens if Black brings his queen over to g6. This manoeuvre is positionally justified as it fights for the e4-square; and as we shall see from the following example it also contains a lot of tactical poison!

Game 22
□ **J.Ripley** ■ **O.Hardy**
Bognor Regis 1963

1 d4 f5 2 g3 Nf6 3 Bg2 e6 4 Nf3 d6 5 0-0 Be7 6 c4 0-0 7 Nc3 Qe8 8 Re1 Qg6 9 Qc2?! (Diagram 3)

Taken by surprise, White first plays a passive move and then follows it up with a howler.

9...Ne4!

Black crushes White's hope of advancing with 10 e4. Now the rook on e1 and the white queen on c2 are all dressed up with nowhere to go.

 TIP: If you don't know what to do in the Classical Dutch as Black, stick a knight on e4. The chances are that it is the best move on the board.

10 Nxe4??

Still, there was no reason for White to blunder. In fact, this is just the sort of thing that happens when a player is surprised by a sharp, unknown variation. You can bet White wouldn't have fallen apart like this if he had faced nine moves of Queen's Gambit theory.

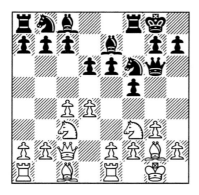

Diagram 3 (B)
White prepares e2-e4

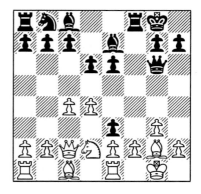

Diagram 4 (W)
A glorious end for Black's f-pawn

10...fxe4 11 Nd2 e3! 0-1 (Diagram 4)

White resigned as he loses a rook after 12 Qxg6 exf2+. It is for glorious moments such as this that we play the Dutch.

WARNING: If you intend to play this variation as White you had better be careful!

An Important Tactic

It appeared that White was following a logical plan in Game 22 but then came to a sudden positional dead end. In fact, from Diagram 5 it may have looked sensible to prepare e2-e4 with 9 Qc2, but it was a wasted move, which gave Black time to frustrate him with 9...Ne4.

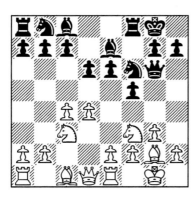

Diagram 5 (W)
Can White play e2-e4 here?

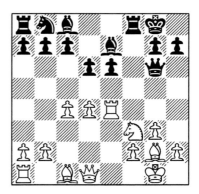

Diagram 6 (B)
The rook is 'poisoned'

In fact, Black's control over the e4 square is illusory. White can play 9 e4! fxe4 10 Nxe4 Nxe4 11 Rxe4 **(Diagram 6)** and Black can't play 11...Qxe4? because of 12 Nh4! trapping his queen in the centre of the board! White therefore achieves his positional aim of advancing e2-e4 and now exerts pressure on the backward pawn on e6.

The following game illustrates White's chances once he achieves this central breakthrough.

Game 23
☐ **Y.Yakovich** ■ **S.Dyachkov**
Maikop1998

1 d4 e6

Remember, this is the most solid move order!

2 Nf3 f5 3 g3 Nf6 4 Bg2 Be7 5 0-0 0-0 6 c4 d6 7 Nc3 Qe8 8 Re1 Nc6 9 e4 Nxe4 10 Nxe4 fxe4 11 Rxe4 Qg6

Okay, there is no flashy pseudo-rook sacrifice with this move order, but the game position could also be reached after 8...Qg6 9 e4! fxe4 10 Nxe4 Nxe4 11 Rxe4 Nc6.

12 Qe2

The alternatives include 12 Re1 or 12 Re3, in both cases keeping a slight edge. Black's best response would be to build up towards ...e6-e5 as in the game.

12...Bf6

Black not only prepares to advance in the centre but also readies himself to answer d4-d5, which can be a nuisance with the knight on c6 in this type of position, with the solid ...Ne5.

13 Bd2 e5 (Diagram 7)

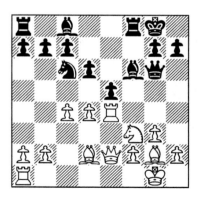

Diagram 7 (W)
Black plays ...e6-e5

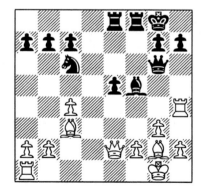

Diagram 8 (W)
...Rad8 was stronger

If Black doesn't play this advance then all he can do is sit and watch passively as White probes away for the next 50 or so moves. For example if 13...Bd7, 14 Bc3!? planning 15 Rae1 etc.

14 dxe5 dxe5!?

Black submits to an isolated pawn. Contrary to first impressions, in this type of centre it is normally a good idea. A centre pawn is still a centre pawn, no matter how vulnerable, and as such controls key squares. Here it keeps the white knight out of the d4-square. It also blocks the e-file, which obstructs the white queen and rook on e4. These are two highly important functions.

Instead, after 14...Nxe5 15 Nxe5 Bxe5 16 Bc3 Bxc3 17 bxc3 Bd7 Black would even have the better of the pawn structure, but it is an open question whether White can exploit his (temporary) control of the e-file and a possible discovered attack on the b7-pawn.

15 Bc3 Bf5 16 Nh4!

An excellent move. Black is forced to part with one of his bishops, which diminishes his counterplay and gives White the long-term advantage of the bishop pair.

16...Bxh4 17 Rxh4

Everything is going swimmingly for White, apart from the fact that he now has this rook on an odd square. Can Black use this fact to activate his game?

17...Rae8? (Diagram 8)

It soon becomes clear that Black pins his hopes on *direct* action against the rook on h4 with the plan of ...Qf6 and ...g7-g5. However, rather than trying to capture the errant castle, he should have aimed *indirectly* to exploit the rook's offside position by taking control of the open file in the centre with 17...Rad8!. If then 18 Bxc6?, 18...Qxc6 19 Qxe5 Rf7 would give Black huge compensation for the pawn in view of his light square domination.

18 Qe3!

White prevents the active 18...Nd4.

18...h6 19 b4!

The threat of b4-b5 is very disruptive.

19...Qf6 20 b5 Nd8

There is no time to trap the rook as if 20...g5 then 21 bxc6! gxh4 22 cxb7 looks crushing for White: the passed pawn will sooner or later cost Black the exchange leaving him with a wrecked pawn structure.

21 c5! (Diagram 9)

White creates a way out for his rook as 21...g5 was now really a threat.

21...c6 22 Ra4

So Black didn't manage to corner the white rook. Therefore, White has the chance to exploit his long-term positional plusses: the two bishops, the chance to put pressure on the queenside and the target on e5.

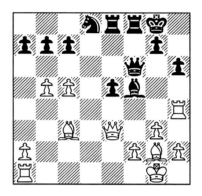

Diagram 9 (B)
Offering c4 for the rook

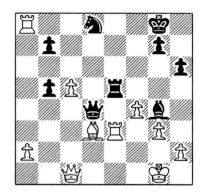

Diagram 10 (B)
A winning position for White

22...cxb5 23 Rxa7 Rf7 24 Ra8 Rd7 25 Re1 Rd3 26 Qc1 Bg4

There was no good way to prevent White's next move. The pin on the back rank and the weakness on e5 mean that Black is strategically lost, but he still manages to conjure up an attack that might have confused a lesser or nervous opponent.

27 f4

At last White wins material. He has to be a little careful as he has loosened his kingside somewhat.

27...Qf7 28 Bxe5 Qd7 29 Bf1 Rxe5!?

A last gamble.

30 Bxd3!

And not 30 fxe5? Qd4+ 31 Kh1 (31 Re3 Rd1 32 Qc3 Bh3!) 31...Bf3+ 32 Bg2 Bxg2+ 33 Kxg2 Qd5+ 34 Kg1 Qd4+ with a draw.

30...Qd4+ 31 Re3! (Diagram 10)

The attack ends with Black forced into a losing endgame.

31...Rxe3 32 Rxd8+ Qxd8 33 Qxe3 Kf7 34 Qe4 Qd7 35 Kf2 Be6 36 a3 Bd5 37 Bxb5!

There goes another pawn.

37...Qxb5 38 Qxd5+ Ke7 39 Ke3 Qb2 40 Qe5+ 1-0

Black Opposes e2-e4 with ...Qh5

After 7 Nc3 Qe8 it makes a lot of sense to play 8 Qc2, rather than 8 Re1, as it prepares e2-e4 all the same and doesn't give Black any chance to block the e4-square with ...Ne4. However, lacking a rook on e1, White is exerting less direct pressure down the e-file, and so Black can afford to play energetically with 8...Qh5!?. The positional justification for this move is revealed in the notes to the following game.

Game 24
☐ **J.Werle** ■ **A.Dgebuadze**
Groningen 2002

---

1 Nf3 e6 2 c4 f5 3 d4 Nf6 4 g3 Be7 5 Bg2 0-0 6 0-0 d6 7 Nc3 Qe8 8 Qc2 Qh5!?

I like this move here. However, it is less promising if White has played 8 Re1 as after 8...Qh5 9 e4 there is no 9...e5 trick. This is fully explained in the notes to Game 26.

9 b4?

This bid to gain space on the queenside isn't appropriate here as White has been gearing up towards e2-e4. Still, after the immediate 9 e4?! e5!! **(Diagram 11)** Black has achieved his beloved pawn centre on e5 and f5, and if 10 dxe5 dxe5 11 exf5 (11 Nxe5 fxe4 leaves the white knight on e5 awkwardly placed) 11...Bxf5 the dynamism of the black pieces outweighs the structural weakness of the isolated pawn.

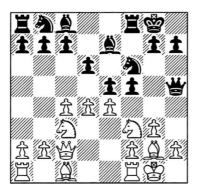

Diagram 11 (W)
9...e6-e5!!

Diagram 12 (W)
Coming to f7

Instead of the game continuation 9 b4? or 9 e4?!, White can play in more restrained, and better, style with 9 b3 when after 9...a5 10 Bb2 Na6 11 Rae1 c6 12 a3 Bd8 13 e4 it looked like White was going to get a clear positional advantage in Flohr-Kotov, USSR Championship 1949. However, once again the pawn block on e5 allowed Black to generate counterplay: 13...e5!, which Jan Pinski describes in his *Classical Dutch* book as 'a really cool pawn sacrifice'. Black is neither submitting to dull positional inferiority after 13...fxe4 14 Nxe4 nor allowing White to over run his centre with 14 e5. The game continued (after 13...e5!) 14 dxe5 dxe5 15 Nxe5 Nc5 and now Pinski suggests that White should try 16 Bf3 Qh3 17 exf5 Bxf5 18 Qd1 Bc7 19 Bg2 with advantage. I think that 16...Ng4! looks a better way for Black to pursue his attack, for example 17 Nxg4 fxg4 18 Bg2 Ne6! and the knight heads to g5 or possibly d4 to give a very dangerous check on f3.

TIP: Don't worry, you aren't expected to memorise all this analysis or understand everything about it. The aim is simply to reinforce the value of the ...e6-e5 advance in your mind so that you might apply it in a similar situation in one of your own games, rather than automatically concede the centre with ...f5xe4.

9...Nc6!

Black responds in precise style. Normally I would tell you that ...Nc6 is a bad idea before going ...d6-d5, as White can split up the black centre with the reply d4-d5!, when Black has no time to bypass the d5-pawn with ...e6-e5 because his knight is hanging. However, in this actual position 10 d5? drops the b4-pawn. Therefore, thanks to his opponent's inaccuracy, Black is able to get his knight from b8 to an active square on f7 without being punished.

This sort of error scenario occurs all the time in games by players not quite in the chess genius league, which is why when choosing an opening you should consider 'how much scope does it give my opponent to go wrong?' as well as 'what is the theoretical assessment?' Remember that Kramnik and other creators of theory are immensely well prepared and rarely make opening inaccuracies; therefore a dynamic but risky line will often fail against them. On the other hand, the same line can prove deadly against players outside the top echelons of chess.

10 a3 Nd8! (Diagram 12)

The black knight escapes before White gets the chance to carry out his positional threat with 11 d5!.

11 Bb2 Nf7 12 e4 e5!

Thanks to the knight on f7, this advance is well supported.

WARNING: Under no circumstances must White be allowed to advance e4-e5 in the centre as this will give him a crushing space advantage. As soon as White plays e2-e4 the pawn must be eliminated or, perhaps better still, blocked in its tracks.

13 dxe5 dxe5 14 Nd5

White tries to reassert some control in the centre as 14 exf5 Bxf5 leaves Black with all four minor pieces active – a rare luxury after 14 moves.

14...Bd8!

A common reaction to Nd5 in the Classical. Black has no wish to give his opponent counterplay down the c-file after 14...Nxd5? 15 cxd5.

15 Nxf6+

One of the good points about having the black queen on h5 is that she indirectly defends the e5 pawn, for if 15 Nxe5? then 15...Nxe5 16 Bxe5 Ng4 costs White a piece in view of mate on h2.

15...Bxf6 16 Rfe1 f4! (Diagram 13)

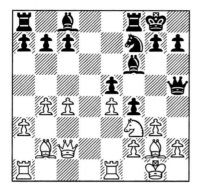

Diagram 13 (W)
16...f5-f4!

Diagram 14 (B)
No perpetual check

You will meet this move many times in the Leningrad Dutch (Chapters 7 and 8). Black opens the diagonal for his bishop on c8, blocks a frontal attack on the e5-pawn, threatens to build up a massive wedge of pawns with ...g7-g5 followed by ...g5-g4 (White has to worry about it, whether Black actually chooses to play like this or not!) or simply plans ...f4xg3 to further his attack by opening the f-file. However, as a rule Black wouldn't hurry to carry out this last exchange, the threat being stronger than the execution. After ...f4xg3, f2xg3 White might be able to use the f-file for defence or counterplay with Rf1 etc, or support his second rank more easily against an attack.

17 gxf4

Hoping to seize the initiative after 17...exf4? 18 e5 or better still 18 Bxf6 gxf6 19 Qd2, but Black pursues his attack.

17...Bh3!

Now the white kingside rapidly collapses.

18 Nxe5 Bxg2 19 Kxg2 Nxe5 20 Bxe5 Bxe5 21 fxe5 Qf3+ 22 Kg1 Rf4

It looks all over, but White finds a way to limp on painfully for another 19 moves.

23 h3 Qxh3 24 Re3 Rg4+ 25 Rg3 Rxg3+ 26 fxg3 Qxg3+ 27 Qg2 Qxe5 28 Rd1 Rf8 29 c5 Qe6 30 Rd3 h6 31 Rg3 Qe5 32 Rg6 Kh7 33 Rg4 Rd8 34 Qe2 Qc3 35 Rg2 Qc1+ 36 Kh2 Rd1 37 Rxg7+ (Diagram 14)

The last try, but there is no perpetual check.

37...Kxg7 38 Qg4+ Kf7 39 Qf5+ Ke7 40 Qe5+ Kd7 41 Qf5+ Ke7 42 Qe5+ Kd7 0-1

The king can go to c6.

Game 25
□ **K.Spraggett** ■ **L.Comas Fabrego**
Platja d'Aro 1994

1 d4 f5 2 g3 Nf6 3 Bg2 e6 4 c4 Be7 5 Nf3 0-0 6 0-0 d6

NOTE: Here Classical Dutch expert and grandmaster Kevin Spraggett is forced to play White against his favourite opening. Most players hate to take on their own brain child, and even if they know how to beat it they don't want to show the whole world.

7 b3

It would be simplistic to imagine that White's only plan versus the Classical Dutch is a rapid e2-e4. Here, rather than hurrying to force through e2-e4, White gives himself the option of putting pressure on the black centre with Bb2 or even Ba3. If now 7...Qe8 8 Nc3 Nc6? White has the chance to undermine the black centre with 9 d5!, for example 9...exd5 10 cxd5 Ne5 11 Nd4 and most of the energy has vanished from Black's position. As we saw at move nine in the previous game, ...Nc6 is a luxury Black can only afford if he can neutralise the reply d4-d5 in a tactical manner.

7...Qe8 8 Nc3

Nor is the white knight always destined to go to c3, as for example 8 Bb2 a5 9 Nbd2 might be played. However, the knight exerts less pressure on the centre on d2 than c3, so White can at best hope for a transposition to the normal Nc3 moves after engineering e2-e4. In this particular instance, Black can profit through playing 9...Nc6! without having to fear the d4-d5 move of the previous note (he can just take it). Instead after 10 a3 Bd8 11 Ne1 e5 Black achieved his desired pawn centre in Averbakh-Boleslavsky, Zürich 1953.

8...a5 (Diagram 15)

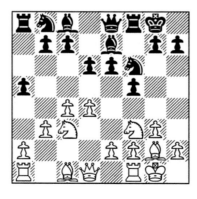

Diagram 15 (W)
The restraining ...a7-a5

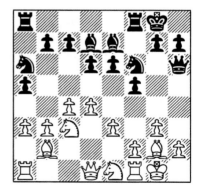

Diagram 16 (W)
A queen swap? No thanks!

This is a very useful move. Since White hasn't committed himself to action in the centre with e2-e4, the restraint of a possible white queenside pawn expansion is a good idea. More specifically, because of the drawback to ...Nc6, Black intends to develop his knight on the alternative square a6. Here it may look passive, but it reinforces Black's control over b4. Not infrequently the knight gets to jump into b4 with effect, especially when it blocks out a white bishop on a3 or attacks a white queen on c2. In both cases the support of a pawn on a5 will often prove essential.

9 Bb2

The more direct, and possibly stronger, 9 Re1 occurs in the next game.

9...Qh5

Pinski points out that Black had an interesting alternative plan in the shape of queenside action, beginning with 9...Na6 10 e3 (or 10 a3 c6, limbering up for ...b7-b5) 10...Rb8 11 Re1 Qh5 12 e4 Nxe4 13 Nxe4 fxe4 14 Rxe4 b5! with dynamic play.

10 e3

This quiet move consolidates the white centre. Besides helping to deter a future ...f5-f4 pawn advance, it clears the way for the manoeuvre Ne2 and Nf4, hitting both the black queen and e6. However, it can't be considered to be as challenging for Black as a scheme based on e2-e4.

10...Na6 11 a3 Bd7 12 Ne1

Here we see another purpose to White's tenth move: it seems that Black is obliged to exchange queens, as b7 is hanging.

12...Qh6!? (Diagram 16)

This is the move all Dutch players would like to make as it keeps the tension, whilst something like 12...Qxd1 13 Rxd1 c6, although perfectly okay for Black, doesn't exactly set the pulse racing.

13 Qe2?!

Quite understandably White avoids the critical 13 Bxb7, when he comes under a heavy attack, e.g. 13...Ng4 14 h4 g5 (14...Bxh4!?) 15 Bxa8 gxh4 (15...Rxa8!?) 16 Bg2 hxg3 17 Nf3 Bh4!? 18 fxg3 Bxg3 19 Re1 Bf2+ 20 Kf1 Bxe1 21 Kxe1 Nxe3 and the attack goes on. It often happens that after spending a long time looking at a sharp variation, a player ducks the challenge and then selects what seems a solid alternative without too much thought.

Putting the queen on e2 appears sensible, but in fact it turns out to be a waste of time as White never manages to engineer the e3-e4 advance. Much more to the point was 13 Nd3!, for example 13... Ng4 (to provoke a weakness on h3; 13...c6 was the alternative) 14 h3 Nf6 15 b4 with pressure on the queenside.

WARNING: Beware of making natural-looking moves in the Dutch.

13...c6 14 Nd3

Now Black snatches the chance to create counterplay in the centre before White can advance with b4 and b5 on the queenside.

14...e5! 15 dxe5 Ng4

The double attack by the knight on e5 and h2 often proves handy for Black when he has his queen on the h-file. See for example the glorious Bogoljubow-Alekhine encounter in the next chapter (Game 31).

16 h3 Nxe5

The knight takes up a strong centre post and its exchange with 17 Nxe5 dxe5 gives Black his much-desired mobile pawn centre. White is left to rue the fact that he moved his queen to e2, as if she were still on d1 then 17 Nxe5 would now win a piece!

17 Na4?!

White is anxious to be rid of the black knight, but his own knight is walking into a dead end. Instead the modest 17 f4 Nxd3 18 Qxd3 Nc5 19 Qc2 was called for.

17...Nxd3 18 Qxd3 Be6

Sidestepping the threat of 19 Nb6.

19 Bc3 Nb8

It appears that White is doing the attacking, but the black knight is happy to be forced backwards as it is en route to replace its comrade on e5.

20 f4

White sensibly puts a guard on e5 and also rules out any tricks with ...f5-f4 intending ...Bxh3.

20...Nd7 21 e4?

White undoes the good work of his previous move, as h3 will figure as a target again. He is continuing to strive for the initiative but how can it be right to open the centre when his knight is offside on a4?

WARNING: If you lose your opening advantage as White, don't carry on playing as if you still stand better. Learn to put the brakes on, as a draw is better than a loss!

21...Rae8! (Diagram 17)

Black completes his centralisation, and by defending e7 introduces the threat of 22...fxe4 23 Qxe4 Bxh3, as the bishop on e7 would no longer hang to the white queen. White is therefore forced to advance the h-pawn, which leaves a big hole on the g4-square.

22 h4 fxe4 23 Bxe4 Bh3 24 Rfe1 Bf6! 25 Bxf6

A very interesting moment. I assume both players thought that the pawn on d6 was taboo because after 25 Qxd6 Black can capture on c3 with 25...Bxc3?!, and then upon 26 Qxh6 he can save the bishop with the zwischenzug 26...Bd4+. However, looking a bit further after 27 Kh2 gxh6 28 Rad1!, White is more or less holding his own in the tactics. Much more challenging is the exchange sacrifice 25...Rxe4!? 26

Rxe4 Qg6! when White loses after 27 Re3?? Qc2. The only way to avert mate on g2 is by blocking on d2, but it will cost the rook on a1: 28 Qd2 Qxd2 29 Bxd2 Bxa1. Still, White can hold on with 27 f5! Bxf5 28 Re3 Bg5!? 29 Qxf8+! (this time the zwischenzug is a killer after 29 Qxh6? Bxe3+) 29...Nxf8 30 hxg5 Ne6 when Black has only the slightly better chances in this imbalanced position.

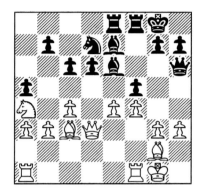

Diagram 17 (W)
Black is centralised

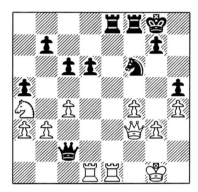

Diagram 18 (W)
Securing g4 for the knight

NOTE: Zwischenzug is a German word meaning 'in between move'. When working out variations in your mind, always check to see if a necessary recapture can be profitably delayed for a move.

25 Bxf6 Nxf6 26 Bh1

The bishop should have gone to f3 straightaway.

26...Qh5!

If now 27 Qxd6 then 27...Qg6! hits g3, when 28 Kh2 Ng4+ wins the queen. White also drops his queen after 27 Nc3? Qc5+ 28 Kh2 Ng4+ 29 Kxh3 Nf2+. This means that 27...b5! is now a big threat as the white knight wouldn't be able to retreat without allowing the fatal check on c5.

27 Bf3 Bg4 28 Kg2 Bxf3+ 29 Qxf3 Qf5!

Black has a decisive advantage because of the passive white knight and the huge light square holes in the white kingside. But if Black exchanged queens with 29...Qxf3+?? 30 Kxf3, then suddenly White would have a serious plus in the endgame: his king would be well placed and he could target the weak pawn on d6.

TIP: If you have the initiative, keep the queens on the board; if you are under attack, try to exchange them.

30 Rad1 Qc2+ 31 Kg1 h5! (Diagram 18)

A brilliant attacking move, which creates a base on g4 for the black knight.

TIP: Never underestimate the value of pawns in an attack.

32 Qc3 Qf5! 33 Rxe8 Rxe8 34 Re1 Rxe1+ 35 Qxe1 Qc2 36 Qe6+ Kh7 37 Qe3

The white queen on her own cannot shore up the kingside. If only the white knight could give her just a little help!

37...Ng4 38 Qf3 Kh8 39 Nb6?

After sitting passively on a4 for most of the middlegame, the knight finally stirs – and is instantly captured. However, White was already lost: against other moves, the simplest plan for Black might have been to advance the d-pawn down the board to the queening square with 39...d5 etc. as the white queen could never capture on d5 on account of a check on f2 and then mate on h2.

39...Qc1+ 40 Kg2 Qd2+ 0-1

After the forced 41 Kg1, Black wins the unfortunate knight with 41...Qd4+.

The following game shows why the ...Qh5 idea is far less impressive if White gears up for e2-e4 with Re1.

Game 26
□ **E.Inarkiev** ■ **A.Obukhov**
Krasnoyarsk 2003

---

1 d4 f5 2 g3 Nf6 3 Bg2 e6 4 c4 Be7 5 Nf3 0-0 6 0-0 d6 7 b3 a5

Despite the praise I heaped on this move in the game above, personally I would prefer to seize the chance for 7...Ne4!?, as played in the next game.

8 Nc3 Qe8 9 Re1

More aggressive than 9 Bb2. After a little queenside interlude White redirects play into the standard centre clash.

9...Qh5

Here again I think Black should consider blocking the centre with 9...Ne4, when if 10 Qc2 then 10...Qg6 puts us back into the territory of Game 22, while 10 Bb2 gives Black a choice of moves, of which 10...Na6!? looks interesting.

Chess is a funny old game. In Game 24 I was extolling the virtues of the 'dynamic' 8...Qh5. Here, however, in an almost identical situation, I consider the queen thrust as just leading to a passive game for Black. But it all makes sense as after...

10 e4

Black can't play 10...e5? in the style of Game 24 as he just drops a pawn: 11 dxe5 dxe5 12 exf5 Bxf5 (unfortunately this doesn't attack a queen on c2 here) 13 Nxe5. Therefore Black has to exchange on e4: but what is his plan afterwards?

10...Nxe4 11 Nxe4 fxe4 12 Rxe4 (Diagram 19)

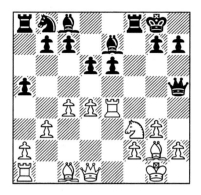

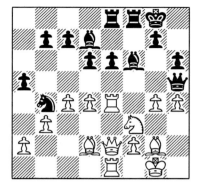

| **Diagram 19 (B)** | **Diagram 20 (B)** |
| A small but lasting edge | An original approach |

Black is of course far from lost here but I think Pinski's remark in his book on the Classical sums it up best: '(White's) superiority might not be overwhelming, but it is practically eternal'. There is no way to be rid of the weakling on e6. If Black had played 9...Qg6 then at least he gets to activate his position with the ...e6-e5 trick.

12...Na6 13 Bf4

Now White simply builds up against the e6-pawn, like a spider patiently wrapping thread around its victim.

13...Bf6 14 Qe2 Bd7 15 Re1 Rae8

Nevertheless, Black is solidly entrenched and can resist the pressure on e6: White won't be able to force a win merely by putting pressure on e6. He needs to open a second front to exploit the greater mobility of his pieces – but how? Inarkiev comes up with a bold solution.

16 h4!

It looks as if this is solely played to obstruct the idea of ...g7-g5 which, though double-edged, would at least give Black counterplay. However, it will soon be seen that there is another purpose behind this move.

16...h6 17 Bd2!

White hits the a5-pawn and so gains time to implement his plan.

17...Nb4 18 g4! (Diagram 20)

A highly original idea: normally it is Black who pushes his g-pawn forwards in the Dutch! However, White has judged that the black pieces are ill placed to resist a direct attack.

18...Qg6 19 g5! Bd8

After 19...hxg5 20 hxg5 the way is clear for 21 Nh4 etc. gaining more time for the attack by harassing the black queen.

20 gxh6 Bc6

If 20...gxh6 then 21 Ne5! dxe5 22 Rg4 Bg5 23 Bxg5 is decisive.

21 Rxe6!

White forces the win with a well-calculated combination.

21...Bxf3 22 Qxf3 Rxe6

Of course if 22...Rxf3 simply 23 Rxg6 wins.

23 Rxe6 Qxe6 (Diagram 21) 24 Qxf8+!!

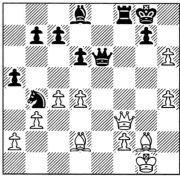

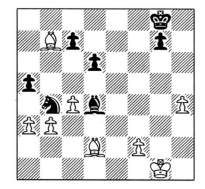

Diagram 21 (W)
Time for a queen sacrifice

Diagram 22 (B)
Takes time, but White wins

The point of White's play. The queen sacrifice to create an unstoppable passed pawn reminds me of Alekhine's famous brilliancy versus Bogoljubow, given in the next chapter, though this isn't quite so fine.

24...Kxf8 25 h7 Bf6 26 h8Q+ Qg8 27 Qxg8+ Kxg8 28 Bxb7 Bxd4 29 a3 (Diagram 22)

So, as in the Alekhine game, brilliancy leads to an endgame which is easily winning, but takes some time. No one likes to resign when there are three drawing havens in view: an opposite-coloured bishop endgame, multiple pawns down, if White unwisely exchanges his dark-squared bishop for the knight; elimination of all the white pawns for Black's pawns, with his knight thrown in as a free gift, as two bishops versus one bishop is a theoretical draw without pawns; or, finally, in the far distance, White has the h-pawn and the light-squared bishop, Black has nothing but a bare king on h8, and they agree a draw.

Needless to say, these havens are all mirages when facing an opponent who has played so brilliantly for the first 29 moves.

29...Nc2 30 Bxa5 Bb6 31 Bc3 Nxa3 32 Be4 Bc5 33 Kg2 Kf8 34 f4 c6 35 Kf3 d5 36 cxd5 cxd5 37 Bxd5 Nb5 38 Be5 g6 39 Kg4 Be7 40 Be4 Kf7 41 Bd5+ Kf8 42 Be4 Kf7 43 Bc6 Nd6 44 b4 Nc8 45 Bd5+ Kf8 46 b5 Bd8 47 Be6 Nb6 48 Bd4 Ke7 49 f5 Kd6 50 Bf7 1-0

After 50...gxf5+ 51 Kxf5 the h-pawn sails through, as if 51...Bxh4 then 52 Bxb6.

Black Plays a Quick ...Ne4 versus Everything

In the games above we saw Black's plan of ...Qe8 followed by ...Qh5 or ...Qg6. White can claim a positional edge having achieved the e2-e4 advance, but Black undoubtedly has his chances – it was just unlucky that he was up against strong grandmasters in two of these games, who were both on top form and didn't do anything to lose tactical or strategical control of the position.

Nonetheless, this method of play isn't to everyone's taste. A radically different approach is possible for Black. He can leave his queen on d8 and aim for a set-up involving ...Ne4, ...Bf6 and possibly ...d7-d5. The move ...a7-a5, which restrains White from queenside expansion with b2-b4 move, may also be part of the system. Such a piece and pawn deployment puts a firm barrier in the way of White's e2-e4 advance.

In effect, Black wants to cherry pick all the best features of the Stonewall, Leningrad and Classical. Thus with ...Bf6 he gets his bishop onto the Leningrad Dutch diagonal. Belatedly perhaps, but the loosening ...g7-g6 has been avoided (as well as numerous theoretical sidelines peculiar to the Leningrad Dutch). As White often plays b2-b3 or b2-b4 to gain space on the queenside, the appearance of the bishop on f6 is annoying, to say the least.

Game 27
□ **P.Tregubov** ■ **C.Bauer**
Clichy 2004

1 d4 e6 2 c4 f5 3 Nf3 Nf6 4 g3 d6 5 Bg2 Be7 6 0-0 0-0 7 b3 Ne4!
(Diagram 23)

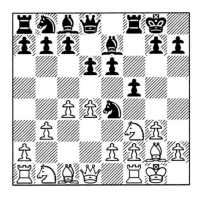
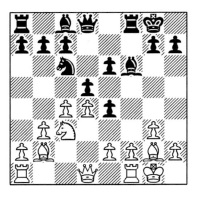

Diagram 23 (W)	Diagram 24 (W)
An early ...Ne4	Planning ...Nc6-e7-f5

Here we have the Classical knight...
8 Bb2 Bf6

...and now we have the Leningrad bishop

9 Nfd2 d5

...and finally the Stonewall centre!

TIP: In the Classical you should always be looking out for a good moment to play ...d6-d5 and switch to a Stonewall type structure – and perhaps thereafter dissolve the centre.

10 Nxe4 fxe4 11 Nc3 Nc6! (Diagram 24)

Excellent! In the usual Stonewall set-up Black would have played ...c7-c6 already, so that his knight could only come out a narrow way via d7. This would be the case if Black played the routine 11...c6 here. Instead, Black sees he has the chance to put his knight on e7 and then f5. It happens with gain of time as d4 is hanging.

12 e3 Ne7 13 f3!

Time isn't on White's side. Black has a space advantage in the centre and so only needs to mobilise his queenside pieces to have good chances. White is therefore obliged to taken immediate action in the centre.

13...Nf5

A beautiful square for the knight. It puts pressure on both d4 and e3 and can only be dislodged by g3-g4, which would seriously weaken the white kingside and be strongly answered by ...Nh4.

14 Qd2 Bg5!

Putting the squeeze on the e3-pawn. Now 15 f4 would be an easy way to counter the immediate tactical threat, but strategically speaking after 15...Bf6 White would no longer have any way to undermine e4.

15 Rae1 exf3 16 Bxf3?

The artificial looking 16 Rxf3 was vital in order to add a defender to the e3-pawn, though 16...c5!? still looks a strong reply.

16...c5!! (Diagram 25)

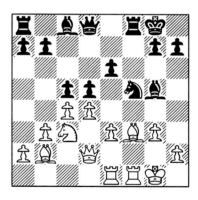

Diagram 25 (W)
Attacking the centre

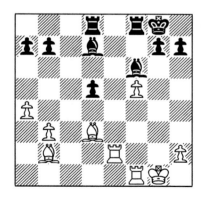

Diagram 26 (W)
Black is winning

The black pawn structure shows ultimate flexibility. If there is a secret to playing the Classical Dutch and Stonewall well as Black, it is knowing when and how to dismantle the centre on your own terms, rather than leaving it as a fixed, rigid structure or letting White detonate it.

Despite the fact that he is playing without his queen's rook and bishop, Black is able to defeat the whole white army thanks to the enormous pressure on d4 and e3. Strategically speaking, it wasn't preordained that this would be the case. Indeed, Tregubov appears still to have been in 'general principles' mode and believed that his lead in development would obviate any tactics. A dangerous delusion, and one that many players fall into when they think they know an opening very well, but then meet with an unexpected move. Intuition isn't always enough. Bauer took the trouble to examine things closely using calculation and came up with the winning idea.

17 cxd5

An unpleasant necessity, as after 17 dxc5 Nxe3! 18 Rxe3 d4 the fork and pin are lethal.

Here we see that White would have done better to put his queen on e2 rather than d2 back at move 14. Oh, the advantage of hindsight! A commentator can be superior to a man of genius if he knows in advance what will happen. Of course, it could be said that in this instance a man of genius like Kasparov would have 'tested' the future after 14 Qd2 by doing a calculation in his head, found it wanting, and so chosen another future with 14 Qe2. But it is terribly hard work to make the correct choice every time, which is why chess has kept its appeal and confounds the greatest minds.

17...cxd4 18 Nd1 dxe3 19 Qd3 Qb6 20 Re2 Bd7

Black holds onto his booty and mobilises his queenside pieces swiftly, thanks to the threat of 21...Bb5, which would spike all three white major pieces.

21 a4 Rad8 22 Be4 Qa6!

With the exchange of queens it's goodbye to any mating chances White might have had against the black king.

23 g4 Qxd3 24 Bxd3 Nh4 25 Nxe3 exd5 26 Nf5

Alas, White can't get his pawn back, as if 26 Nxd5 then 26...Bxg4.

26...Nxf5 27 gxf5 Bf6 (Diagram 26)

And Black, with an extra passed pawn and a target to attack on f5, is winning very easily. It took him until move 53, but there was never any hope for White. It isn't the theme of this book, but it is a nice example of smooth technique. First of all Black exchanges off White's good bishop and one of the rooks – a good idea as two rooks can sometimes cause trouble, whereas one white rook can't do much on its own. Thereafter Black ties his opponent down to three weaknesses: on f5, b3 and h2. Then with the white rook, bishop and king all passive, the black king enters the fray and threatens to shepherd home the passed pawn. This compels White to make a desperate bid for counterplay with his rook, which allows Black to create a second passed pawn and decide the game. Here are the moves:

28 Bxf6 Rxf6 29 Re5 Bc6 30 Rfe1 Kf8 31 Kf2 Re8 32 Rxe8+ Bxe8 33 Ke3 Rb6 34 Bc2 Rb4 35 Kd3 Rh4 36 Re2 Kf7 37 Kc3 a5 38 Bd3 Bd7 39 Re5 Bc6 40 Re2 Rf4 41 Rd2 Kf6 42 Bc2 Rh4 43 Bb1 Rh3+ 44 Kb2 h5 45 Rg2 Be8 46 Rd2 Bc6 47 Rg2 d4 48 Rd2 Ke5 49 Rc2 Bd5 50 Rc7 Rxh2+ 51 Kc1 Rg2 52 Re7+ Kd6 53 Re1 Rg3 0-1

Game 28
☐ **J.Gallagher** ■ **S.Williams**
Port Erin 2001

---

1 d4 f5 2 g3 Nf6 3 Bg2 e6 4 Nf3 Be7 5 0-0 0-0 6 c4 d6 7 Nc3 a5! (Diagram 27)

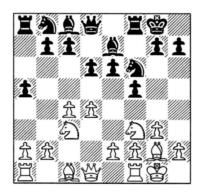
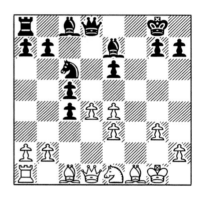

Diagram 27 (W)
That ...a7-a5 move again

Diagram 28 (W)
Attacking White's centre

We have already considered this handy pawn move in Games 25 and 26. Here Simon Williams succeeds very convincingly in proving it is a useful part of Black's strategy. Indeed, by controlling b4 the pawn will provide unexpected assistance to the black minor pieces in the critical variation that occurs in the game.

Nonetheless, Black's 'knight e4 versus everything' strategy begs the question as to whether 7...Ne4!? should be played straightaway. The critical line is then 8 Nxe4 fxe4 9 Ne1 d5 10 f3!. Black's centre is dismantled, but will White inherit a nice pawn centre of his own in its place or a heap of weaknesses? The jury is still out at the time of writing, but things look optimistic for Black if he plays with energy: 10...dxc4! (not 10...exf3 11 Nxf3 when White has a wholesome pawn centre) 11 fxe4 c5! 12 e3 Rxf1+ 13 Bxf1 Nc6 **(Diagram 28)**.

Here GM Ovetchkin points out in *Chess Informant 88* that 14 Bxc4 cxd4 15 exd4 Nxd4 16 Be3 Bf6 17 Nc2 (17 Qd3 b5!?) 17...b5 18 Bxd4 leads to unclear play, while after 14 Nf3 Bf6 15 Bxc4 cxd4 16 exd4 Nxd4 17 Be3 Nxf3+ 18 Qxf3 Qc7 19 Rc1 Qe5 Black already looked better and won after an up-an-down battle and a couple of '??' moves in Filippov-Ovetchkin, Krasnoyarsk 2003.

Rather than trying for an outright refutation of 7...Ne4, White probably does best to settle for a slight edge with 8 Qc2!?, for example 8...Nxc3 9 Qxc3 and now White would have a free hand on the queenside after 9...Bf6? 10 b4, so Black should play 9...a5 before deploying his pieces with ...Nc6 and ...Bf6. Black is solid, if a bit short of space.

Again we see that ...a7-a5 turns out to be a necessary part of Black's strategy. Therefore it is no wonder that Classical Dutch expert Simon Williams elects to play it straightaway.

8 Re1

After 8 Qc2 Nc6! the a5-pawn shows its worth: 9 d5 Nb4 or 9 e4 Nb4 10 Qe2 Nxe4 11 Nxe4 fxe4 12 Qxe4 e5!, intending 13...Bf5, activates Black's game.

8...Ne4!

Williams continues his preventive strategy. Now White is going to have to make some concessions if he wants to achieve e2-e4.

9 Qc2

Anand once tried a different approach to clearing the e4-square with 9 Nd2!?. After 9...Nxc3 10 bxc3 e5 11 e4 f4 12 Rb1 Nc6 13 Nf3 fxg3 14 hxg3, Black gave up a pawn with 14...Bg4 to further his attack but eventually lost after 15 Rxb7 in Anand-Lobron, Frankfurt 1997, though it was by no means clear. Incidentally, I think Anand is the greatest defender of the modern age, as he has shown in many games with Black against Kasparov. So we shouldn't judge the pawn sacrifice too harshly just because it doesn't work against him! Instead Pinski recommends 14...Rf7!?, clearing the f8-square for the queen in order to put more pressure along the f-file.

9...Nxc3

Here Black can speculate with the tricky 9...Nc6? but after 10 Nxe4 Nb4 11 Qb1 fxe4 12 Qxe4 e5 13 dxe5! Bf5 14 Qxb7 Rb8 15 Qa7 Nc2 16 Bd2!, as in Van Wely-Comas Fabrego, Pamplona 1998, Black can take the exchange but his position will still be in ruins.

10 Qxc3

The way is clear for 11 e4, but the white queen has been enticed to a vulnerable square.

10...Nc6

In an earlier game, Simon Williams played 10...c6, which looked harmless but turned out to be a devilish trap after White's obvious reply: 11 e4? (11 c5!? is more circumspect) 11...d5!! and White loses a pawn (12 exd5 Bb4). In the game there followed 12 a3 dxe4 13 Ne5 Bb4!! 14 axb4 axb4 15 Rxa8 bxc3 and White had dropped a lot of material in B.Balogh-S.Williams, Budapest 1994.

WARNING: World Champion Capablanca once remarked that every move has to be checked, no matter how obvious it looks. He was once undefeated for eight years, so listen to his advice!

Well, seven years on Williams doesn't expect to catch grandmaster Gallagher in this trap. Instead he chooses a natural developing move. Nevertheless, if you cast your mind back to the notes to Game 24, you might recall that there can be a downside to the ...Nc6 move: namely d4-d5 undermining the black centre. However, after 11 d5 Bf6 12 Qd2 Ne7 13 Nd4 (White would like to play 13 dxe6 but after 13...Bxe6 the pawn on c4 is a target) 13...e5! (achieving the desired centre) 14 Nb5 Bd7 15 Qc2 h5! 16 Bd2 h4 (Pigusov-Atalik, Beijing 1997) Black's attack on the kingside is more dangerous than anything White can do on the queenside or in the centre.

In this sequence of moves it is easy to miss a crucial role played by the pawn on a5. After 11 d5 Bf6 White put his queen on the awkward d2 square, as if 12 Qc2 then 12...Nb4 13 Qb3 e5 would be very nice for Black (14 a3? Na6 and the knight re-emerges on c5). In contrast, if the black pawn were still on a7 then 12 Qc2 Nb4 13 Qb3 would leave the knight hanging, which means that there would be no time for Black to make the ...e6-e5 advance: he would have to move or defend his knight, after which White has the chance to split up the black centre with d5xe6 when he has a good game.

Another way the pawn would be useful is in harassing the white queen after 11 d5 Bf6 12 Qb3: 12...a4! 13 Qc2 Ne7 14 dxe6 a3! and Black breaks up the white queenside – he can recapture with ...Bxe6 when convenient. Thus we see the dynamism granted to Black's position by the modest looking 7...a5.

Therefore Gallagher carried on with his set plan.

11 e4 e5!

I hope you are starting to get the hang of this by now!

12 exf5

Thanks to the pawn on a5 we don't need to start working out if White can snatch the pawn on e5 or not: after 12 dxe5 dxe5 13 Nxe5?? Black can settle the matter beyond doubt with 13...Bb4!.

12...Bxf5 13 Be3?

White gives away the light squares. He had to play forcefully with 13 dxe5 dxe5 14 c5!, preventing 14...Bb4 and threatening 15 Qb3+ winning the b7-pawn. The position is then murky, with any outcome possible between two tactical players.

13...Be4! 14 Nd2 Bxg2 15 Kxg2 d5! (Diagram 29)

Black suddenly has a wonderful position as 16 dxe5? d4 wins a piece. The white centre is going to collapse after which his king is going to feel distinctly uncomfortable sitting amid all the wide-open light spaces.

16 a3 Bf6 17 Nf3 exd4 18 Nxd4 Qd7 19 Rad1!

TIP: If you have a rotten position, centralise all your pieces – it's best to die with your boots on.

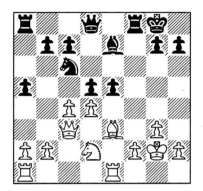

Diagram 29 (W)
Black takes over

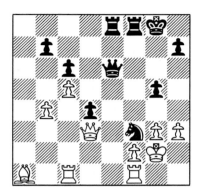

Diagram 30 (W)
Vacating the d5-square

19...Ne5 20 c5 Nf3!

Ouch. The knight shows that White's control of the light squares has become illusory by taking up residence right inside his camp.

21 Rf1 Qg4 22 Qd3 Bxd4 23 Bxd4 Nh4+ 24 Kh1 Nf3 25 Kg2 c6 26 h3 Qe6 27 Be3 g5 28 Bd4 Rae8

As White can do nothing constructive, there is no need for Black to hurry. He therefore brings his last reinforcements into play before starting a direct attack.

NOTE: The disease of a light square weakness quickly spreads to the dark squares, and vice versa. White's inability to eject the black knight from f3 means that he has been unable to use the e1 dark square to challenge for control of the e-file with Rfe1.

29 b4 axb4 30 axb4 Qd7 31 Ba1 Qe6 32 Rc1 d4! (Diagram 30)

This frees the d5-square for the black queen.

33 Rfd1

It would be a dream for White to be able to exchange queens, but 33 Qc4 Qxc4 34 Rxc4 Nd2 costs him the exchange.

33...Rf7 34 Qc4 Qe4 35 Kf1 Nd2+! 0-1

White resigned as he loses one of his monarchs.

White Plays an Early b2-b4

1 d4 f5 2 c4 Nf6 3 g3 e6 4 Bg2 Be7 5 Nf3 0-0 6 0-0 d6 7 b4

This is a dangerous plan for Black to face. White intends to build up on the queenside with moves like Nc3, Bb2 and Qb3, combined with a general pawn advance. The battering ram may first crunch into the black pawn structure on c5 or perhaps b6; what is certain is that White intends to push as many pawns as he needs to splinter the black defences on the queenside.

The white pawn advance may seem slow to begin with, but once it gains momentum it is capable of crushing everything in its path.

Game 29
□ **D.Dumitrache** ■ **S. Williams**
Montpellier 2003

1 d4 e6 2 c4 f5 3 g3 Nf6 4 Bg2 Be7 5 Nf3 0-0 6 0-0 d6 7 b4 Ne4!?

Here's what might happen if Black plays too passively: 7...Qe8 8 Nc3 Nbd7?! 9 Qb3 h6 10 c5! d5 11 Nb5 Bd8 12 Bf4 c6 13 Nd6 Qh5 14 b5 and White dominates the central dark squares and has a strong attack on the queenside. Black, meanwhile... has a queen on h5.

Black's 'play ...Ne4 versus everything' strategy seems the best approach. It is consistent with the classical precept that a wing attack should be met with vigorous action in the centre.

8 Bb2 a5!?

On the other hand, this move might well upset the chess purists. It seems to go against the well known adage that you shouldn't try to play actively on your weaker side, as it will only open up lines for your opponent's pieces. However, Black isn't ready to concede he is weaker on the queenside, despite White's aggressive intentions: he therefore makes a bid to wrest the initiative there.

WARNING: General principles are there to aid your chess understanding, not control it.

9 b5 a4! (Diagram 31)

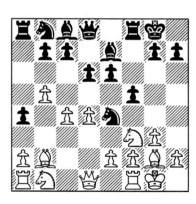

Diagram 31 (W)
A plucky a-pawn

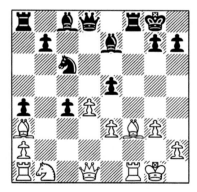

Diagram 32 (W)
Black provides the answer

Black spends another precious tempo on the plucky a-pawn. From a *static* point of view it is isolated and vulnerable on a4, but it has great *dynamic* value.

You may have noticed that the b5-pawn, the proud spearhead of the white attack on the queenside, is being steadily deprived of friends. The black pawn on a4 prevents White playing a2-a4 himself; furthermore, it denies the white queen the b3-square where she would not only support the b5-pawn but also be well placed for a sudden attack on e6 after c4-c5.

10 Nfd2

White aims to be rid of the knight on e4. Instead after 10 a3 c6 White must either capture on c6 or be left with a loose pawn on b5 after the exchange ...c6xb5, c4xb5.

10...d5!

Black refuses to oblige as after 10...Nxd2 11 Nxd2 his dynamism has evaporated. The white bishop on g2 would then enjoy a wonderful diagonal and the Romanian Grandmaster could settle down comfortably to the task of exploiting his space advantage. In contrast, after the game move, even if White gains an objective advantage it is sure to be an untidy, double-edged affair with a strong tactical element. White won't be able to relax for one moment or dare to rely on general principles.

TIP: It can't be stressed enough that in the Classical Dutch Black must always be thinking about setting up a Stonewall Centre.

11 Nxe4

This turns out to be too ambitious as White is neglecting his c4-pawn. Glenn Flear recommends either 11 Ba3 or 11 Na3 on the *ChessPublishing.com* website.

11...fxe4 12 Ba3 c6

Williams continues with his plan of liquidating the white queenside pawns.

13 f3?

Now White drops a pawn. He could bail out with 13 Bxe7 Qxe7 14 bxc6 bxc6 15 Nd2 but even here I think Black has a definite edge (perhaps even 15...e5!? is possible). Note that the pawn on a4 is even playing a useful role here in stopping White from playing Nb3.

13...exf3 14 Bxf3 dxc4!

TIP: Black must always be willing to play ugly-looking moves in the Dutch.

If Black tries to keep an intact centre then White will have the chance to develop his knight on b1 and then fix the black pawns as long-term targets.

15 bxc6 Nxc6

White's pawn storm has swept through the centre and queenside like a tornado, and left a lot of litter in its wake: but whose structure has been damaged the most?

16 e3 e5! (Diagram 32)

A decisive answer to the question of the previous note. Black frees the bishop on c8 and at the same time ensures that White's pawn structure will be just as disjointed as his own. As Black has an extra pawn and the white kingside is flimsy, he has great winning chances. Psychologically speaking it has been a depressing affair for White and it is no wonder he rapidly falls apart.

17 d5 Nb4 18 Nc3 Bh3 19 Bg2 Bxg2 20 Rxf8+ Qxf8 21 Kxg2 Nd3 22 Bxe7 Qxe7 23 Rb1 Qg5!

Black gives back the pawn to gain a decisive attack on White's open king.

24 Rxb7 Rf8 25 d6 Qxe3 26 d7 Ne1+ 27 Kh3 Qh6+ 28 Kg4 Qe6+ 0-1

29 Kh4 Ng2+ 30 Kh5 Qg6 mate is humiliating.

Chapter Six

Classical Dutch: Various Alternative Ideas

 **White Plays Nh3**

 **Black Plays ...Bb4+**

 **White Avoids g3**

White has tried a variety of alternative methods to the Classical main line, notably by avoiding the fianchetto on g2. For his part, Black has often rebelled against the notion that he should put his bishop on e7 and then shut it in, and has preferred to play more actively with ...Bb4+. The present chapter examines all these ideas.

White Plays Nh3

This is close in spirit to the Classical main line. A typical sequence is **1 d4 f5 2 g3 Nf6 3 Bg2 e6 4 Nh3 Be7 5 0-0 0-0 6 c4 d6 7 Nc3 (Diagram 1)**

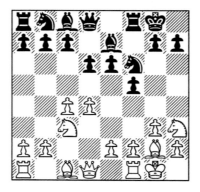

Diagram 1 (B)	Diagram 2 (W)
White plays Nh3	No prospects on h3

This wing development of the knight is one of the most testing responses to the Stonewall and the Leningrad but here it is pretty harmless. If the white knight ever goes to f4 it can be kicked away by ...e6-e5; if it stays on h3 then it risks being cut off from the centre by the same ...e6-e5 move. In the Stonewall, where Black is already committed to ...d7-d5, the knight can go to f4 with little danger of being kicked away by a 'healthy' ...e6-e5 move; its only enemy in the Stonewall is ...g7-g5, but this can be double-edged for Black.

From the diagram, **7...c6!?** is a useful preparation for the ...e6-e5 move as it prevents a future Nf4-d5 as well as blocking the attack on b7, so that the recapture ...Bxf5 becomes an option after **8 e4 e5 9 dxe5 dxe5 (Diagram 2)**.

Here the discomfort of the knight on h3 and the latent dynamism of Black's set-up fully compensates for the potential isolated pawn on e5. Not many players as White would want to bring the bishop on c8 alive with 10 exf5 Bxf5.

TIP: Remember a hole in the pawn structure or an isolated pawn is only a weakness if the opponent can exploit it.

Instead of 10 exf5, the game Greet-Williams, Scarborough 2004 continued

10 Qe2

Black is also very comfortable after 10 Qxd8 Rxd8.

10...fxe4 11 Nxe4 Bf5 12 Nhg5 Qe8 13 Nxf6+ gxf6! (Diagram 3)

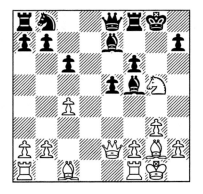
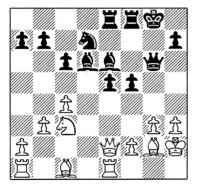

Diagram 3 (W)
Connecting the pawns

Diagram 4 (W)
A strong centre

The correct recapture, as it gets rid of the isolated pawn and gives Black a pair of strong, mobile pawns. Furthermore, the g-file can be utilised to start an assault against the white king.

14 Ne4 Qg6 15 h3 Be6 16 Kh2 f5 17 Nc3 Nd7 18 Re1 Bd6 19 b3 Rae8 (Diagram 4)

And here Black has a strong centre, all his pieces well placed and the chance to attack down the g-file with the general scheme of ...Rf7, ...Rg7 and then ...h5-h4. In the game Black eventually wore down his opponent.

Despite the verdict that Nh3 isn't dangerous, I want to show you a highly instructive and beautiful win as White by former world champion Anatoly Karpov. This is partly to redress the fact that this chapter contains a lot of great wins by Black: I want you to be confident, but don't go thinking that the Classical is a forced win for Black!

Game 30
□ A.Karpov ■ N.Short
Linares 1992

1 d4 f5 2 g3 Nf6 3 Bg2 e6 4 Nh3 Be7 5 0-0 0-0 6 c4 d6 7 Nc3 Qe8

Here 7...c6!? is discussed above.

8 Nf4 g5? (Diagram 5)

Again 8...c6 would be a useful move. The pawn lunge ...g7-g5 is a common theme in the Stonewall: Black aims for counterplay even at the cost of loosening his kingside. The advance ...g6-g5 is also seen in the Leningrad Dutch as part of an attack on the white king. So why is it bad here? It looks all the more attractive as it drives the white knight backwards. Of course, it must have some merits or else Nigel Short, who at the time of this game was on the road to a world championship match with Kasparov, wouldn't have chosen it.

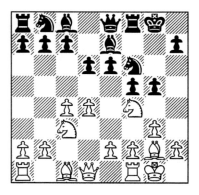

Diagram 5 (W)	**Diagram 6 (B)**
Black lunges with ...g7-g5	Imposing a bind

It is all a question of centre stability. In the Stonewall, Black has set up a solid wall of pawns to stifle action in the centre. Therefore he can sometimes afford the luxury of playing ...g7-g5 as White can't rip open the centre and take advantage of the holes it creates.

The same reasoning applies in the Leningrad. The move ...g6-g5 comes into its own when White has a weak or passive position, or has perhaps committed his pieces to a far off action on the queenside; under these circumstances ...g6-g5 can galvanise a kingside attack. On the other hand, if the white position is strong, and he is able to hit back in the centre, then it can be a terrible mistake.

Returning to the specific situation in this game, we have to ask ourselves whether the centre is stable enough to justify ...g7-g5. All becomes clear after the next couple of moves.

9 Nd3 Qg6 10 f4! h6 11 d5!

The black pawn structure is being undermined on the e6- and g5-squares, and looming on the horizon is the positional threat of e2-e4. With his centre under so much pressure, it is inconceivable that Black will be able to carry out a kingside attack. Therefore the 9...g5 move must be considered to be worse than useless.

11...Na6

Black finds virtually the only way to develop his queenside without dropping material.

12 b4! (Diagram 6)

Karpov has been given the chance to impose a bind on the black position, after which he can start displaying his remorseless technique. Completely wrong would be 12 dxe6? (hoping for 12...Bxe6? 13 Bxb7), as Black can respond 12...c6! followed by ...Bxe6 or even ...Nc7 and Nxe6, when all White has done is freed Black's queenside minor pieces.

12...exd5 13 Nxd5!

The only consistent move: White refuses to let the situation in the centre stabilise with 13 cxd5.

13...Nxd5 14 Bxd5+ Kh7

Now Black is ready to strengthen his centre with 15...c6 16 Bg2 Nc7 and then 17...Be6, and so White must strike at once.

15 b5! Nc5

Perhaps the best chance to hold on was with the humble 15...Nb8.

16 Nxc5 dxc5 17 Qc2

White's winning plan begins to take shape. He intends to open up all the lines in the centre and then hit the f5-pawn with as much force as possible. This will expose the black king to a fatal attack, or failing that, it will cripple the ability of the black pieces to function properly.

17...a6 18 a4 Rb8 19 fxg5 hxg5 20 Ra3!

The rook enters the fray in the most economical manner.

TIP: Don't assume that the only way to develop a rook is sideways along the first rank.

20...c6 21 Bg2 Bf6 22 Be3! (Diagram 7)

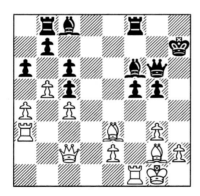

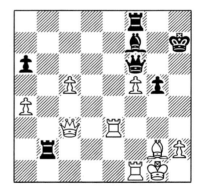

Diagram 7 (B)	Diagram 8 (B)
Hitting c5	Killing all counterplay

The threat to c5 will force Black to part with his strong defensive bishop.

22...Bd4 23 Bxd4 cxd4 24 e3! dxe3 25 Rxe3

Now that there are big wide-open spaces in the centre, Black must surely wish his g-pawn were back on g7.

25...Be6 26 g4!

Excellent: the black king has been hiding on h7 behind his queen, thinking it to be the safest place on the kingside; but Karpov finds a way to turn this arrangement to his advantage as there is a potential pin with Be4.

26...Rbe8 27 bxc6 bxc6 28 c5! Qf6

Black loses at least a pawn with a rotten position after 28...Bc8 29 Rxe8 Qxe8 30 gxf5.

29 Bxc6 Rb8 30 gxf5 Bf7 31 Bg2 Rb2 32 Qc3! (Diagram 8)

The offer to exchange queens kills off the black counterattack.

32...Qxc3 33 Rxc3 Rd8 34 c6 Rdd2 35 Be4 Re2 36 c7 Rxe4 37 c8Q 1-0

A fine example of the 12th world champion's fantastic strategical play. Incidentally, a couple of weeks after this game was played Anatoly Karpov and Nigel Short sat down to play a match to decide who would challenge Kasparov for the world title. The Englishman struck back to win 6-4 and thus achieve the greatest result of his career. Every player of the black pieces needs a similar ability to bounce back from disaster, as there are sure to be some nasty drubbings in his Dutch career – as well as hopefully some great wins!

Black Plays ...Bb4+

In the Classical main line, Black puts his king's bishop on e7, and then shuts it in with ...d7-d6. He waits patiently for the chance to activate the bishop on f6 or elsewhere in the future. However, many players prefer to play more directly with ...Bb4+, which has the merit of getting the bishop outside of the pawn chain before playing ...d7-d6.

An Attempt to Confuse the Opponent

It is normal to wait for White to play c2-c4 before checking on b4, although 1 d4 f5 2 g3 Nf6 3 Bg2 e6 4 Nf3 Bb4+!? **(Diagram 9)** is interesting.

At first glance this appears to be a silly move that just drops a tempo, but on the other hand it has been played more than once by David Bronstein and Bent Larsen, as well as opening expert Ludek Pachman and Dutch devotee Robert Bellin!

If 5 Bd2?! Black is very happy to exchange dark-squared bishops with 5...Bxd2+ rather than have his bishop enclosed in e7. This facilitates the plan of ...d7-d6, ...0-0 and ...Nc6 (and ...Qe8 if necessary) to force through the freeing move ...e6-e5.

After 5 Nbd2 Black can be pleased to have ruled out ideas of Bg5 by White, and, as we shall see in the Bogoljubow-Alekhine game, the knight is less effective on d2 than it would have been on c3 after c2-c4 and Nc3: it is obstructing White's pressure on the centre and so facilitating the ...e6-e5 equalising move. On the other hand, Black still has to work out what to do with the bishop, which is out on a limb on b4. GM David Bronstein once successfully tried ...Bxd2!? as soon as White castled: he gave up the bishop pair but had freedom of action for his other pieces.

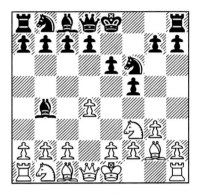

Diagram 9 (W)
A confusing check

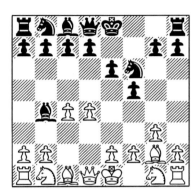

Diagram 10 (W)
Check!

The key reply is of course 5 c3, though as White is going to have to play c3-c4 to put pressure on the centre, he isn't gaining any time by taking advantage of the 'silly' check on b4. When confronted with the check on b4, the great Serbian GM Gligoric simply played 5 c3 Be7 6 0-0 0-0 7 c4 d6 8 Nc3, reaching the Classical main line.

So it seems that 4...Bb4+ might well just transpose to the main line. It's certainly worth a try to confuse the opponent!

Now let's look at the main line with ...Bb4+:

1 d4 f5 2 c4 e6 3 g3 Nf6 4 Bg2 Bb4+ (Diagram 10)

It isn't possible to introduce you to the Classical Dutch without showing you the following brilliant game. It is the most famous game ever played in the Dutch and a candidate for the title of best game ever played.

Game 31
☐ **E.Bogoljubow** ■ **A.Alekhine**
Hastings 1922

1 d4 f5 2 c4 Nf6 3 g3 e6 4 Bg2 Bb4+ 5 Bd2

Black had an active position after 5 Nc3 0-0 6 Nf3 Bxc3+ 7 bxc3 d6 8 0-0 Nc6 9 Ba3 Ne4 10 Qd3 Qf6 11 Ne1 Qg6 in Pliester-Glek, Breda 2000. White misses the pressure that the knight on c3 normally exerts in the Classical main line.

Instead 5 Nd2!? aims to show that the bishop is badly placed on b4. It will have to be exchanged for the knight, when White has the two bishops. But are they worth anything special? Take the following example: 5...0-0 6 Ngf3 d6 7 0-0 Bxd2 8 Bxd2 Qe7 9 Bc3 (to deter the freeing move 9...e5) 9...Nc6 10 d5 Nd8 11 dxe6 Nxe6 12 e3 (evidently White avoided 12 Nd2 in view of 12...f4 with an attack) 12...Ne4 13 Qc2 Bd7 14 Nd4 Qf7 15 b3 Rae8 and Black's strong central build up ensured him equality in Rowson-Motwani, Hamilton 2004. Back at move nine in this sequence, if 9 Qb3 then 9...a5!? is interesting, so that 10 Rac1 Nc6 11 d5 Ne5 keeps the black knight in the centre as White has no tricks based on Nxe5 followed by Bb4.

5...Bxd2+

Black can change his mind and return the bishop with 5...Be7. Then after 6 Nf3 c6 7 0-0 0-0 8 Nc3 d5 White is in the Stonewall, having been deprived of plans involving b2-b3 and Ba3. Black has had to put his bishop on e7, rather than the usual Stonewall square d6; but on the other hand the bishop is out of the way of White's Bf4 move, which is the natural plan now that he is deprived of Ba3, and also makes Bg5 a less attractive option (there's no pin on the knight on f6).

A possible continuation is 9 b3 Qe8 10 Ne5 Nbd7 11 Nd3 Ne4 12 Be1 Bf6 13 e3 b6 14 Rc1 Bb7 15 Ne2 Rc8 16 Bb4 (at last White finds an active role for the bishop, but Black's game is well established now) 16...Be7 17 Bxe7 Qxe7 18 Re1 c5 19 cxd5 exd5 20 dxc5 bxc5 with complex play in P.Braun-A.Dgebuadze, Bad Wörishofen 1999

Alternatively, Black can keep the centre fluid: 6...0-0 7 0-0 d6 8 Nc3 Qe8 9 Re1 Qg6. In the Classical main line (1 d4 e6 2 c4 f5 3 g3 Nf6 4 Bg2 Be7 5 Nf3 0-0 6 0-0 d6 7 Nc3 Qe8 8 Re1 Qg6) White has the trick 9 e4 fxe4 10 Nxe4 Nxe4 11 Rxe4 breaking through in the centre as the rook is immune – 11...Qxe4 12 Nh4 traps the black queen. But in the line here, with the white bishop on d2, Black can just take the rook and say thank you very much as 10 e4 fxe4 11 Nxe4 Nxe4 12 Rxe4 Qxe4 13 Nh4 can be met by 13...Qxd4 or 13...Qd3.

So White is deprived of the idea of 9 e4. The position is highly interesting and little known. If 10 Qb3 or 10 Qc2 then 10...Ne4!? looks a good answer. Note that the bishop on d2 blocks White from playing the useful move Nd2 to help evict the black knight from e4.

6 Nxd2?!

If the position is of a quiet nature, it is usually better to develop the pieces to their best squares, rather than throw them into battle as quickly as possible. Here 6 Qxd2 followed by 7 Nc3 would allow White to impose pressure on the centre.

6...Nc6 (Diagram 11)

Now nothing can prevent Black from freeing his game with an eventual ...e6-e5. Alexander Alekhine was way ahead of his contemporaries in the art of opening preparation and already has the initiative as Black after only six moves.

7 Ngf3 0-0 8 0-0 d6 9 Qb3

Already Bogoljubow is floundering around for a decent plan. After 9 Qc2 e5 10 dxe5 dxe5 11 e4 f4!? Black has attacking chances.

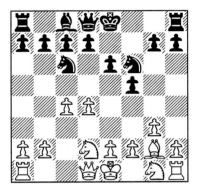

Diagram 11 (W)
Preparing ...e6-e5

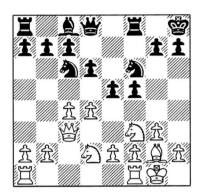

Diagram 12 (W)
Tactics allow ...e6-e5

9...Kh8 10 Qc3 e5! (Diagram 12)

Rightly showing contempt for his opponent's 'plan'. If White takes twice on e5 he drops the knight on d2, which means he has failed to prevent Black activating his game.

11 e3

Now White will be acting on the defensive for the rest of the game.

11...a5!

This common pawn thrust is normally explained in defensive terms, namely that before setting in motion a kingside attack Black wants to restrain White from starting a queenside pawn action with b2-b4. However, it is also frequently an attacking move: Black is greedy for control of the whole board, and plans active operations on the queenside. You can see a similar 'board wide' strategy in the game between Fritz and Anand in Chapter Eight (Game 49).

It is also interesting to recall that Alekhine, when asked to define his chess style, remarked that the desire to play on both sides of the board was one of his character traits. In this game he achieves this in exemplary style. It is no wonder that he regarded this game as one of the two finest he had ever played (the other game was against Réti at Baden-Baden in 1925; incidentally, both games were with Black).

12 b3 Qe8

For the moment Alekhine sets his sight on a kingside attack.

13 a3 Qh5!

More skulduggery keeps the e5-pawn alive, for if 14 dxe5 dxe5 15 Nxe5?? then 15...Nxe5 16 Qxe5 Ng4 costs White his queen in lieu of mate on h2. Now White has to reckon with ideas such as ...f5-f4 fol-

folhttp://www.dandbpublishing.com/layout.htmllowed by ...Bh3 and
...Ng4. Of course, Black need not hurry into a committal line of play
and could bring up reinforcements with 14...Bd7 and ...Rae8, etc. Bogoljubow therefore tries to clear the decks for his pieces on the kingside with a series of pawn moves.

14 h4 Ng4 15 Ng5 Bd7 16 f3 Nf6

Now the threat is 17...f4, when the g3 point collapses allowing Black
to wreck White's kingside with ...Qxh4.

17 f4 e4 18 Rfd1 h6 19 Nh3

White has prevented the collapse of his kingside, but the pawn structure has resolved itself in a way highly unfavourable to him. The
bishop on g2 will be blocked in for the rest of its existence. Furthermore, the pawn on g3 is vulnerable and there is a hole on g4. So, in
view of White's weaknesses along the g-file, are we to expect a direct
assault there by the maestro of attacking play, involving the doubling
of rooks on the g-file and the advance ...g7-g5?

No. White has a bishop on g2 and a knight on h3 doing nothing – but
if Black started an attack on the kingside, both pieces could become
heroes. There is no reason at all for Black to help the white pieces
find useful roles. Therefore the correct strategy for Black is to open
lines on the queenside, so that the white bishop on g2 and to a lesser
extent the knight on h3 remain spectators.

**TIP: If you want to start an attack, open lines as far away as possi-
ble from the main body of the opponent's army.**

19...d5! (Diagram 13)

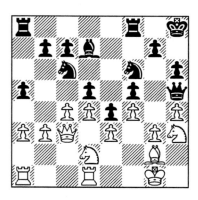
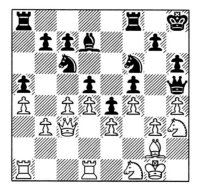

Diagram 13 (W)	Diagram 14 (W)
Undermining the queenside	Planning ...Nb4

A fine positional move that begins to undermine the foundations of
the white queenside. It also chokes any counterplay White might have
gained by playing d4-d5 himself. You will notice in what follows that
the black bishop on d7 is an active helper in Black's battle for queen-

side supremacy, whilst the white bishop on g2 is nowhere to be found.

20 Nf1

White is naturally loath to play 20 c5 when play could go 20...a4 21 b4 Na7, and Black is ready to invade along the light-squared diagonal with a sequence such as ...Bb5, ...Bd3 and then ...Nb5.

20...Ne7 21 a4

This doesn't help much as the pawn is a target on a4, but if 21 c5 then 21...Bb5 as above, while 21 Nf2 a4! 22 b4 dxc4 23 Qxc4 Ned5 leaves the black knight in dreamland on d5.

TIP: A knight is often superior to a bishop if it can sit on a centre square without any danger of being driven away by an enemy pawn.

Having read the tip above, which square do you think is now beckoning the black knight on e7?

21...Nc6!! (Diagram 14)

Alekhine shows excellent flexibility of thought. White's best move would now be 22 a3 if it were legal, which just shows how carefully you should treat each pawn move – there's no going back once you have committed the foot soldiers.

22 Rd2 Nb4

On this post the knight can never be challenged by a white pawn, or indeed a white piece, unless White came up with a fantastical manoeuvre to get a knight to c2 or a2. The black knight therefore dominates the queenside and is ready to leap into d3.

23 Bh1

White can only pretend that he is about to generate counterplay with Rg2, Nf2 and g3-g4.

23...Qe8!

Meanwhile the black queen joins in a very real attack on the queenside light squares.

24 Rg2 dxc4 25 bxc4

White gives up a pawn to preserve some semblance of control over the centre, as after 25 Qxc4 Nfd5 (one of the many good moves available) followed by 26...b5! etc. Black will conquer all the light squares.

25...Bxa4

Now Alekhine has won a passed pawn and the rest, as they say, is a matter of technique – which just happens to include a queen and double rook sacrifice!

26 Nf2 Bd7 27 Nd2 b5! 28 Nd1 Nd3! 29 Rxa5 b4 30 Rxa8 (Diagram 15) 30...bxc3!!

As a matter of fact, after 30...Qxa8 31 Qb3 Qa1! (with the threat of 32...Ba4) and then ...Ra8 as necessary, it is likely that Bogoljubow would have resigned in around another five moves. After the game continuation he manages to fight on for another 23 moves. Normally the rule is that you should try to finish the game in as quick and efficient manner as possible. However, a player who loved chess as much as Alekhine couldn't resist the beautiful game continuation.

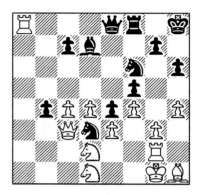

Diagram 15 (W)
Brilliant and beautiful

Diagram 16 (W)
A final queen offer

31 Rxe8 c2 32 Rxf8+ Kh7

The notorious weakness of the knight against pawns is well demonstrated here. You can bet that a pair of bishops wouldn't have let the passed pawn slip through them!

33 Nf2 c1Q+ 34 Nf1 Ne1

After all the hullabaloo Black has a queen for two rooks, and the handy threat of 35...Nf3 mate. White's pieces are too badly coordinated to offer much resistance and Black soon wins the exchange to be up on material as well as position.

TIP: The health of White's king's bishop is a useful barometer of his chances in the Dutch Defence. Here it has spent the crucial part of the middlegame shut in on h1. No wonder everything went wrong for White.

35 Rh2 Qxc4

Perhaps even stronger was 35...Nc2! followed by 36...Nxe3 to create a passed pawn as soon as possible.

36 Rb8 Bb5 37 Rxb5 Qxb5 38 g4 Nf3+ 39 Bxf3 exf3 40 gxf5 Qe2 41 d5 Kg8 42 h5 Kh7 43 e4 Nxe4 44 Nxe4 Qxe4 45 d6 cxd6 46 f6 gxf6 47 Rd2 Qe2! (Diagram 16)

The final queen offer of the game!

48 Rxe2 fxe2 49 Kf2 exf1Q+ 50 Kxf1 Kg7 51 Kf2 Kf7 52 Ke3 Ke6 53 Ke4 d5+ 0-1

TIP: A good way to improve your feel for an opening is to play through so-called model or textbook games. In these games a well-informed player uses the laws of positional chess to outplay an op-

ponent who puts up little or no resistance.

There are seldom such one-sided encounters between modern grandmasters: a strong player will do all he can to muddy the waters with complications if he sees that the logical course of the game will lead to his defeat.

The games of yesteryear are a very fruitful field for model games: the loser might be a world-class player, but nevertheless he fell into a bind because his generation was unaware of a positional subtlety, which later became commonplace knowledge among strong players. It is instructive to see a great chess mind struggling with unknown problems.

It is also more interesting playing through a famous game of the past than seeing how a modern grandmaster thrashed an amateur in a simultaneous display or in the first round of a 'Swiss' tournament.

Don't neglect to study the games of the past!

White Avoids g3

Here we consider a variety of ideas for White: 1 d4 e6 2 c4 f5 3 Nc3 Nf6 4 Qc2; 1 d4 e6 2 c4 f5 3 Nc3 Nf6 4 Nf3 Be7 5 Bf4 and 1 d4 e6 2 c4 f5 3 Nc3 Nf6 4 f3. Note that 1 d4 f5 2 Nf3 Nf6 3 Bg5 e6 has already been discussed in Chapter 2.

Game 32
□ **E.Agrest** ■ **S.Williams**
Port Erin 2004

1 d4 e6 2 c4 f5 3 Nc3 Nf6 4 Qc2 Bb4 (Diagram 17)

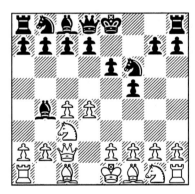

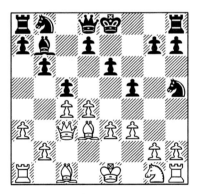

Diagram 17 (W)
The Nimzo Move

Diagram 18 (W)
Planning ...Qh4+

In the fianchetto variation of the Nimzo-Indian, Black often makes use of the ...f7-f5 pawn advance to fight for control of the e4-square, for example 1 d4 Nf6 2 c4 e6 3 Nc3 Bb4 4 e3 b6 5 Bd3 Bb7 6 Nf3 Ne4 7 Qc2 f5 8 0-0 Bxc3 9 bxc3 0-0. This comparison teaches us two things: firstly, that the bishop fianchetto on b7 is a good idea for Black in this type of pawn structure; and secondly, that thanks to the Dutch move order, Black has already played ...f7-f5 without needing to move the knight out of the way to e4, where it can be undermined by f2-f3. Indeed, as will be seen, Dutch players have found that after White plays f2-f3 to control the e4 square, the reply ...Nh5!? is highly interesting. Of course, if the knight were on e4 it couldn't get to h5 in one go!

The comparison with the Nimzo-Indian isn't all one-way traffic in Black's favour. The fact that Black has played ...f7-f5 has encouraged aggressive players of White to indulge in attacking plans involving g2-g4. This latches onto the f5-pawn as a means of levering open the b1-h7 diagonal and the g-file as a prelude to an all-out attack on the black king. It is assumed in this scenario that the white king will castle queenside or stay in the centre.

5 e3 b6 6 Bd3 Bb7 7 f3 c5 8 a3 Bxc3+ 9 Qxc3 Nh5!? (Diagram 18)

The aforementioned knight manoeuvre. If now 10 Ne2, 10...Qh4+ is annoying for White, who must either forfeit the right to castle or play 10 g3, when the f3 barrier against the bishop on b7 is loosened.

10 Nh3 Qh4+ 11 Nf2 d6 12 dxc5 bxc5 13 b4

White has a dark-squared bishop with no rival, which is a definite long-term advantage. The absence of the black queen and knight on h5 from the centre means that White can hope for a telling breakthrough along the b-file or perhaps for fatal pressure against d6.

So strategically things are rosy for White, but he is facing a potential attack on the kingside and this can't be ignored. It is all a question of whether Black can generate enough dynamism to outweigh the unfavourable strategic outlook. It won't matter if he loses on the queenside and in the centre if a short-term tactic leads to mate on the kingside.

13...Nd7 14 Be2 0-0 15 0-0 Rf6! (Diagram 19)

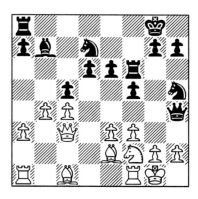

Diagram 19 (W)
Going for broke

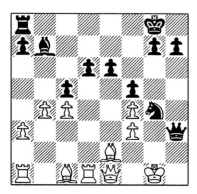

Diagram 20 (W)
A decisive attack

Black must go for broke on the kingside before his centre is dismantled with Bb2, Rad1 and Rxd6.

16 Nh3?

White loses his nerve. Even the strongest players become anxious when facing an attack. He should have continued calmly with 16 Nd3! when if 16...Rh6, 17 Qe1! is a very disagreeable offer to exchange queens. White would be in charge after 17...Qe7 18 e4!, discovering an attack on the rook on h6, while the trick 17...Nf4? fails to 18 exf4! Qxh2+ 19 Kf2 Qh4+ 20 Ke3 and the king is sitting pretty on e3. White could also defend sufficiently after 16...Rg6 17 bxc5 Qg5 18 Rf2, with chances to pursue his initiative on the other wing.

As often happens, looking deeply into a position confirms the value of a general rule known to all but the least experienced players: namely that you should centralise your pieces (Nd3!) rather than playing them to the edge of the board (Nh3?).

16...Rg6

Now rather than being an aid to the white king's defences the knight on h3 is a target that helps Black's cause, for of course if 17 Qe1? Qxh3, while after 17 Kh1 Black can exploit the power of the bishop on b7 with 17...Rxg2!! 18 Kxg2 Qg4+ 19 Kh1 Qxh3 (Black even has the luxury of forcing a draw with 19...Ng3+ if he wishes) 20 Qe1 Ne5! 21 Qf2 g5!! 22 Qg2 Qxg2+ 23 Kxg2 g4 etc. with a rampaging attack.

17 Nf4 Rh6 18 Nh3

Here 18 Qe1 won't do because of 18...Nxf4 when h2 drops as 19 Qxh4 Nxe2+ is a lethal zwischenzug.

18...Rg6 19 Nf4

Back again. Having confirmed that White isn't going to fall into any trap after ...Rh6, this time Williams finds a convincing way to wear down the white defences.

19...Nxf4 20 exf4 Rh6 21 h3 Rg6 22 Kh1 Qg3 23 Rg1 Rh6

The threat is now mate in two with 23...Rxh3+ 24 gxh3 Qxh3 – the so called epaulet mate.

24 Rd1 Nf6 25 Qe1

There is no time for 25 Rxd6 as besides 25...Ne4, which is good enough, Black has 25...Ng4!! when White has no defence against the threat of 26...Rxh3+ 27 gxh3 Nf2 mate (or simply 26...Qh2 mate), for if 26 fxg4 then 26...Qg2 mate (not to mention 26...Qxc3). The bishop sitting on b7 is dictating the outcome of the game from afar.

25...Rxh3+! 26 gxh3 Qxh3+ 27 Kg1 Ng4! (Diagram 20)

Now White has no choice but to give up his queen to avert 28...Qh2+ 29 Kf1 Qh1 mate, as taking the knight allows mate on g2. This has been an amazing demonstration of the power of Black's initiative in the Dutch against careless play by White.

28 Qf2 Nxf2 29 Kxf2 e5 30 Rg1 Qh4+ 31 Kf1 g6 32 fxe5 Qh3+ 33

Kf2 Qh2+ 34 Rg2 Qxe5 35 Ra2 Re8 36 Rc2 Bxf3! 0-1

It is mate on e1 if he takes with the bishop, while 37 Kxf3 Qe4+ costs a rook. A nice finishing touch to a fine game by Simon Williams. Agrest is rated over 2600 but he has been completely blown away.

Game 33
☐ **P.Wells** ■ **A.Summerscale**
Edinburgh 2003

---

1 d4 e6 2 c4 f5 3 Nc3 Nf6 4 Nf3 Be7 5 Bf4

White's thought processes behind this move can be summed up as follows: 'I want my bishop out of the pawn chain before playing e2-e3. I'll put it on f4 in order to deter a counterattack by Black with ...d7-d6 and ...e6-e5. Then, having stabilised the position in the centre to my satisfaction, I intend to start a direct attack on the black king with h2-h3 and g2-g4. It is assumed, of course, that Black will castle kingside.'

The drawback to this reasoning is, firstly, that White is as much provoking a counterattack with ...e6-e5 as deterring it, as it would come with gain of time by hitting the bishop on f4. And secondly, just exactly where is the white king going to live while the attack with g2-g4 is taking place, as White is going to have a fractured pawn structure on both sides of the board?

5...0-0 6 h3 Ne4!

Here Black's beloved ...Ne4 move is the perfect answer to White's attempt to play on the wing.

7 e3

Less ambitious is 7 Qc2 so as to avoid the doubled pawns and keep the queenside as a secure habitation for the white king. Then Black could set up a Stonewall with 7...d5, as the attempt by White to snatch a pawn with 8 cxd5?! exd5 9 Nxe4 fxe4 10 Bxc7? would be suicidal after 10...Bb4+, for example 11 Nd2 Qe7 12 e3 Bxd2+ 13 Kxd2 Rxf2+ 14 Be2 Nc6 15 Bg3 Nxd4! 16 exd4 Qg5+ and 17...Qxg3 etc.

Another option for Black is 7...Nc6!? with counterplay after 8 d5 Nb4. Again it would be foolhardy for White to snatch at material because 8 Nxe4? fxe4 9 Qxe4 d5! 10 Qe3 Nb4 11 Rc1 Nxa2 etc. is tremendous for Black.

7...Nxc3 8 bxc3 d6 9 Bd3 Nc6 10 g4 Bf6 11 gxf5

Both sides have gone purposefully about their business: White has carried out his kingside advance, while Black has built up towards ...e6-e5. It appears that White has got in first and consequently defeated his opponent's plan, as after 11...exf5 all the tension in the centre vanishes. In that case, White could concentrate on his attack down the g-file with very little to disturb him. Any counterattack by Black on the queenside would be at an embryonic stage compared to White's onslaught, which means that White could afford to castle queenside in order to get his queen's rook involved in the attack.

It is moments like these at the end of the opening phase that set the pattern for the middlegame. Will it be a question of dour defence by Black, or will he find a way to keep the dynamism in his set-up?

11...e5!! (Diagram 21)

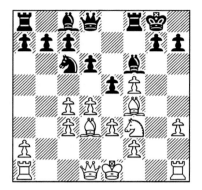

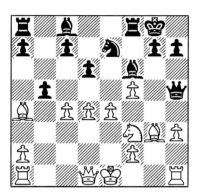

Diagram 21 (W)
Rising to the challenge

Diagram 22 (W)
16...b7-b5!!

Black rises to the challenge. The need to retain active chances is far more important than the immediate recapture of the pawn on f5.

12 Bg3 Qe8!

Now there is a double threat of 13...e4 and 13...exd4 14 cxd4 Nxd4, breaking up White's centre.

13 Bc2 exd4 14 cxd4 Ne7!

Black intends to recapture on f5 with his knight: a far livelier scenario than the stale, prospectless 11...exf5.

15 Ba4!?

An ingenious attempt to hold together the centre.

15...Qh5 16 e4

Visually at least, White's pawn centre is marvellous. However, such a huge chain of pawns requires the close support of its pieces, and here the white army is scattered or inert. Furthermore, the white king is sitting uncomfortably on e1. It won't take much of a nudge for the white centre to come tumbling down...

16...b5!! (Diagram 22) 17 Bc2

The knight on f3 is indefensible after 17 Bxb5 Nxf5! 18 exf5?! Bb7 etc.

17...Nxf5! 18 exf5 Bb7 19 d5 Bxa1

White has avoided disaster on f3 only for it to strike on a1. Now White will remain the exchange down with a ruined centre, as if 20 Qxa1 Qxf3 etc.

20 0-0 bxc4 21 Nd4 Qxd1 22 Rxd1 Bxd4 23 Rxd4 Rae8 0-1

Game 34
☐ **R.Kempinski** ■ **E.Gleizerov**
Stockholm 2000

1 d4 e6 2 c4 f5 3 Nc3 Nf6 4 f3 (Diagram 23)

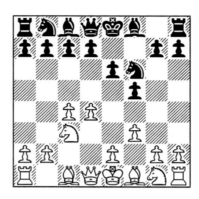

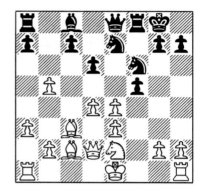

Diagram 23 (B)
Ambitious

Diagram 24 (B)
How should Black recapture?

An ambitious move: White prepares the e2-e4 advance in the most direct manner possible. On the other hand he spends a tempo without developing anything and deprives his knight of its favourite f3-square.

We shall see a similar idea versus the Leningrad, namely 1...f5 2 c4 Nf6 3 Nc3 g6 4 f3. Black has more resources in the Classical version, as his dark-squared bishop can immediately fight for control of e4.

4...Bb4!

This is surely the best reply, though 4...Be7 5 e4 Nh5!? could be tricky as Black can hit and run with ...Bh4+ in order to make White weaken his position with g2-g3.

5 Bd2 0-0 6 a3 Bxc3 7 Bxc3 d6 8 e3 Qe8

Black has conceded the bishop pair, but on the other hand he achieves a comfortable development and soon equalises the balance in space with ...e6-e5.

9 Qd2 Nc6 10 Bd3 e5 11 Ne2 e4

After his methodical build up, Gleizerov decides it is time to try for an advantage by seizing control of the light squares in the centre. He has to proceed carefully as with ...e5-e4 he removes a barrier to White's dark squared bishop, which may appear passive on c3 but can suddenly spring to life after d4-d5.

12 Bc2 b5!

Black continues his plan in forceful style. Having established a light square spearhead on e4, he now makes a fine pawn offer in order to win d5 for his knights.

13 cxb5 Ne7 14 fxe4 (Diagram 24) Nxe4??

A grave disappointment. Gleizerov is tempted to get rid of White's light-squared bishop and undoes all the good work of his opening strategy. He should have played 14...fxe4, planning to put a knight on d5 where it dominates the centre. Then 15 d5? Nexd5 is just good for Black, which means that White's dark-squared bishop has to remain a passive piece. Note that 15 a4 a6 16 bxa6 Bxa6 gives Black good compensation for the pawn, e.g. 17 0-0 Ned5 when it is difficult to see a good plan for White as 18 b4? Bxe2 drops a piece. Black meanwhile can build up with ...Kh8, with ideas of ...Nfg4 attacking e3 etc.

15 Bxe4 fxe4 16 d5!

White should never have been allowed to make this move unless the d5-pawn could be captured, as now the bishop on c3 becomes a monster.

16...Qxb5 17 Nf4 Ng6

Of course if 17...g5? then 18 Qd4 decides the game.

18 Qd4

You can easily verify that this position would be far healthier for Black if he still had a knight on f6 and White a bishop on c2. For one thing there would be no mate threat on g7.

18...Rf7 19 Nxg6 hxg6 20 0-0-0

The opposite-coloured bishops greatly favour White here as his bishop can help the queen attack the key mating point on g7, whereas Black's bishop cannot help besiege b2.

20...Bg4 21 Rd2 Raf8 22 Re1 Qb3 23 Rf2!

Black's control of the f-file proves illusory, as his rook on f7 has to keep the g7-square guarded.

23...Qa2

The queen may look visually impressive here, but she cannot do much by herself. In contrast, the white queen will have the help of all the other white pieces when it comes to striking a blow against g7.

24 Rf4 Bd7 25 Ref1 c5 (Diagram 25) 26 Qxg7+!!

The brilliant culmination of White's kingside build up.

26...Rxg7 27 Rxf8+ Kh7 28 R1f7!

The point: the rook on g7 is paralysed as if 28...Rxf7 29 Rh8 mate.

28...Ba4

Black threatens mate in two, but it is far too late.

29 Rxg7+ Kh6 (Diagram 26) 30 Kd2

Actually Fritz tells me there was a mate in six moves with 30 Rh7+ Kg5 31 Bf6+ Kf5 (or 31...Kg4 32 Rh4+ Kf5 33 g4 mate) 32 Bg7+ Kg5 33 Bh6+ Kg4 (33...Kh5 34 Bf4+ Kg4 35 h3 mate) 34 Rf4+ Kh5 35 Bg7+ Kg5 and you have a choice between 36 Bf6 and 36 h4 mate. I prefer the latter as it is aesthetically pleasing that Black is mated by g2-g4, h2-h3 and h2-h4 in the variations above – the pawns deal the final blow after all the action by the pieces.

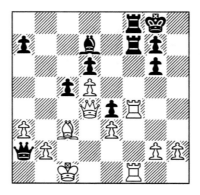

Diagram 25 (W)
White has a brilliant win

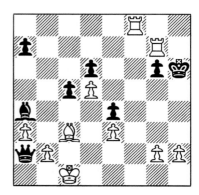

Diagram 26 (W)
A choice of wins

30...Bb5 31 Rh8+ Kg5 32 h4+ Kf5 33 Rh5+!

Just when it seemed the black king might be slipping out, White finds the killer move. If the rook is taken it is mate on g5.

33...Kg4

TIP: Every Dutch player needs a sense of humour.

34 Rg5+ Kxh4 35 Bf6 1-0

There's nothing good to be done about mate with 36 Rh7.

Chapter Seven

Leningrad Dutch: Introduction and Main Line

Introduction

Let's take a look at the opening moves of the Leningrad Dutch.

1 d4 f5 2 g3

The most flexible move: assuming White plans to fianchetto kingside he should do so straightaway. For one thing, it keeps the option of playing Nh3 if Black adopts the Stonewall or Nf3 if he plays the Classical.

Leningrad lines in which White avoids the fianchetto, and all other divergences from the main line, will be considered in the next chapter.

2...Nf6

The black knight is best on f6 in every line I can think of in the Dutch, except perhaps in some lines after 2 Bg5, so bringing it out at once makes sense.

3 Bg2 g6 (Diagram 1)

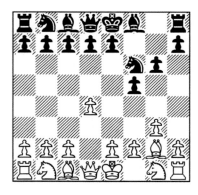 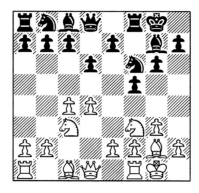

Diagram 1 (W)	Diagram 2 (B)
Both sides fianchetto	The Leningrad Dutch standard position

The kingside fianchetto defines the Leningrad Dutch.

4 Nf3 Bg7 5 c4

White increases his space advantage in the centre.

5...d6

The pawn on d6 fits in well with the fianchetto on g7, as is also the case in the King's Indian Defence. It both stabilises the situation in the centre and is preparatory to ...e7-e5.

6 0-0 0-0

Both kings are sheltered behind the fianchettoed bishop: this is a piece of great defensive and attacking power, which they should be wary of exchanging off.

7 Nc3 (Diagram 2)

We have arrived at the Leningrad main line position. Black now has three main alternatives: 7...Qe8, 7...c6 and 7...Nc6, and these will be the subject of the present chapter.

History

Back in the 1920s and 1930s, many young and ambitious players wanted to create lively, dynamic positions as Black. After 1 d4, the near-universal 1...d5, with its bland diet of Queen's Gambits, could hardly satisfy them.

This urge for adventure led to the development of the so-called 'Indian' defences in which Black fianchettoes on g7: the King's Indian, Grünfeld and Benoni (the Nimzo-Indian was named through its association with these other defences, even though Black plays his bishop to b4 rather than g7). The idea of putting the bishop on g7 eventually spread to the Dutch: after all, if 1 d4 Nf6 2 c4 g6 3 Nc3 Bg7 was an acceptable development for Black, then why shouldn't 1 d4 f5 2 c4 Nf6 3 Nc3 g6 be equally valid?

The Leningrad Dutch, as it came to be known, was developed by a group of masters in that city in the 1940s.

Strategies

There are three musketeers in the Dutch Defence: the Stonewall, Classical and Leningrad.

In the Stonewall Black begrudges White any space in the centre and clamps down on things at once with ...d7-d5. It is a wise player who stops any combinations by the opponent!

Black is more adventurous in the Classical, but still he won't let White have a free hand in the centre: if White plays e2-e4, he will straightaway balance things up with ...e7-e5; or he might prevent e2-e4 altogether by playing ...Ne4 and ...d6-d5.

Now consider the Leningrad Variation. Black not only concedes a space advantage, but also makes no immediate attempt to reclaim his territory. He is satisfied to develop his pieces, leaving White with his centre superiority unchallenged. He trusts that the solid features of his position, notably the bishop on g7 and the pawn bulwark on d6, will allow him to generate counterplay. Naturally such a strategy carries with it the element of risk. If a space advantage didn't mean anything then the laws of strategy would cease to exist!

Therefore, it requires a great deal of alertness and energy to play the Leningrad Dutch, and Black frequently lives on his nerves. He might find his position is collapsing on the queenside, or in the centre, or on the kingside, or perhaps in all three places at once; but he has to show resilience and courage and trust in his counterplay, no matter how bad things appear. Don't forget it's difficult for White as well. He might think he has played all the right moves, which he can justify with logical, convincing arguments – and then he is suddenly mated by an absurd tactic that had no right to be there!

The normal, intuitive rules of chess strategy break down in such complex situations. You can't get away with playing 'obvious' moves – you have to find the move that really offers dynamic chances. Often, a quiet move – let's say ...Kh8 – can be more devastating than a move that shatters the eardrums such as ...Rxf3. Then after the game, when all is calm and peaceful, it can be asserted 'instead of ...Rxf3 giving up the exchange for insufficient counterplay, Black should have played ...Kh8! clearing the g8-square for his rook with a strong attack down the g-file.'

Chess purists might not be pleased with the messy, 'ugly' positions that often result in the Leningrad. Still, we should remember that chess is a sport, and if both players are confused this is a moral victory to Black, who started off with the worse position.

Theoretical?

You bet. Every opening in which a bishop is placed on g7 generates deep theoretical discussions. This is because Black is trying to deprive White of his birthright of a slight opening advantage by making the position complex and double-edged. White cannot tolerate this and so searches out an idea that restores his advantage; Black responds by confusing the issue with another new idea, and so the arms race continues until in some lines it goes way past move 20.

Black's fundamental Aim

We can see from its history that the idea behind the Leningrad came from the King's Indian. Indeed, it *is* the King's Indian, but with the pawn on f5 instead of f7. Black's pawn structure is therefore crying out for the move ...e7-e5. This advance would not only neutralise White's space advantage but also create a wedge of pawns which could become a battering ram against the white kingside. It would add tremendous energy to the black formation.

Black carries out his plan with zero resistance

First of all, take a look at what happens if White plays passively and lets Black achieve his desired aim.

Game 35
□ **J.Ochkoos** ■ **K.Spraggett**
Toronto 2000

1 d4 f5 2 c4 Nf6 3 Nc3 g6 4 g3 Bg7 5 Bg2 0-0 6 Nf3 d6 7 0-0 c6 8 Bf4?

An awful move that makes the bishop a target and so hands over the initiative to Black.

8...Nh5!

Already White has lost control of the position, for if he leaves the bishop on f4 then 9...Nxf4 snaps it off. This would not only deprive him of the bishop pair, but also leave him with a loosened kingside after 10 gxf4, without being able in any case to prevent ...e7-e5 in the long term.

9 Bd2 e5 10 dxe5 dxe5 (Diagram 3)

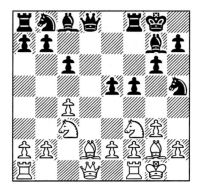

Diagram 3 (W)
The pawn umbrella opens

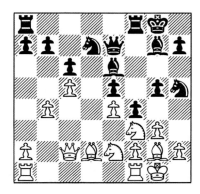

Diagram 4 (W)
A kingside pawn wedge

Already Black has set up the e5/f5 pawn chain which is his heart's desire in the Dutch Defence.

NOTE: Black now has a tremendous version of the King's Indian.

11 e4

White has no wish to allow 11...e4 when his knight is driven back from the centre and the black bishop on g7 enjoys an excellent diagonal.

11...f4!

A very important strategic motif, which occurs regularly in the Leningrad Dutch – a similarly drastic example is seen in Game 42. The f-pawn sidesteps the challenge of the pawn on e4 in order to leave the centre blocked and adds its weight to a pawn storm on the kingside with ...g6-g5 etc. There is also the option of ...Bg4 combined with ...fxg3, in order to open the f-file and put pressure on the knight on f3 which would be pinned against the queen. Note that the black pawn on e5 is performing an important role in fixing the white pawn on e4. If it were still on e7 White might well reply 12 e5 to free the e4-square and create some tension in the centre, even if it lead to the loss of the e5-pawn.

12 Ne2

White has no constructive ideas for counterplay, but this move does contain a strong positional threat: namely 13 Bb4! attacking the black rook on f8 and so gaining time for 13 Qxd8. Black, of course, has no wish at all to exchange queens when he has the makings of a strong attack on the kingside. His next move meets the threat.

13...Qe7! 13 b4 Be6 14 Qc2 Nd7 15 c5 g5! (Diagram 4)

Black has taken the chance to develop his pieces before commencing the attack as White's queenside advances pose no danger to him. But now all is ready for the final assault.

NOTE: The fact that Black has his bishop on g7 means that his king is better guarded than in the Classical or Stonewall. Therefore he has greater scope to advance his kingside pawns without jeopardising his own king's safety.

16 h3 g4 17 hxg4 Bxg4 18 gxf4 Nxf4 19 Nxf4 exf4

Now Black is ready to play 20...Bxf3 21 Bxf3 Ne5 followed by moves like ...Qg5, ...f4-f3, ...Rf6 etc. though it is doubtful there would be any 'etc.' needed once the white king was bombarded by all these pieces. The game now concludes very painfully for White.

20 e5 Bxf3 21 Bxf3 Nxe5 22 Qb3+ Kh8 23 Rfe1 Rad8 24 Rxe5 Qxe5 25 Rd1 Rxd2 0-1

White restrains ...e7-e5 and prepares e2-e4

The game above demonstrates the potential of the Leningrad to sweep White off the board if he loses control. Therefore, he has to meet it very carefully and precisely. A natural plan for White is to manoeuvre to prevent ...e7-e5 and then play e2-e4 himself, say after Re1. This would not only dispose of the f5-pawn (it is assumed Black would have to play ...fxe4 and White would recapture Nc3xe4) but also leave the e7-pawn backward. Black's hopes for a pair of mobile kingside pawns would be gone forever and he would be left with static weaknesses, including the hole on e6.

Let's see how the world's greatest master of restraint goes about the task as White.

Game 36
□ **A.Karpov** ■ **V.Malaniuk**
Moscow 1988

1 d4 f5 2 g3 Nf6 3 Bg2 g6 4 c4 Bg7 5 Nf3 d6 6 0-0 0-0 7 Nc3 Qe8 (Diagram 5)

A very useful move in the Leningrad. The black queen not only supports the ...e7-e5 advance, but can go to f7 as in the game, or – in the future after an advance of the kingside pawns – to g6 or h5 to assist in a kingside attack.

8 b3

We saw that White had no luck with Bc1-f4 in the previous game. A fianchetto development is much superior as the bishop gets to influence matters in the centre from a distance, without being vulnerable to attack by pawns.

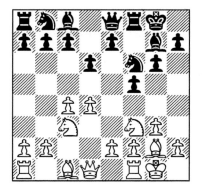

Diagram 5 (W)	**Diagram 6 (W)**
The typical ...Qe8	A controversial position

8...Na6

Well, no doubt you are now thinking that everything I said above is nonsense, as GM Vladimir Malaniuk, the world's leading authority on the Leningrad, declines the chance to play the wonder move ...e7-e5.

Philosophically speaking, the reason many of us have a love-hate relationship with chess is that it refuses to abide by a logical set of positional rules. Whilst we know for certain that a bishop will always move diagonally, no matter how complicated the position, the strategical laws are rules of thumb: mere approximations to the truth that at times can mislead us completely.

As a matter of fact, the position after 8...e5 9 dxe5 dxe5 10 e4! Nc6 **(Diagram 6)** is a controversial one.

Some years ago I wrote a book on the Leningrad and recommended that White investigate 11 Nd5 Qd7 12 Ba3 Rd8 13 Qc2!?, which I believed to be good for him. It seemed to me that he would get dangerous threats down the d-file. Theory marches on, and the latest word at the time of writing is 13...Nxe4 14 Rad1 Kh8 15 Ne7 Nd4! 16 Nxd4 exd4 17 Bxe4 fxe4 18 Qxe4 Qg4 19 f4 Qe6 20 Qxe6 Bxe6 21 f5 (G.Flear-Bauer, Montpellier 2003) leading to an endgame which Glenn Flear considers at *ChessPublishing.com* to be about equal. So at the moment the ball is back in White's court as he has to find a way to prove that 8...e5 isn't an equalising move.

It isn't the purpose of this book to bombard you with deep analysis, but from the above discussion you will probably have gathered why 8...e5 isn't automatically a good move. It leads to a full-blooded struggle taking place along the open d-file, with White playing active moves like Ba3 and Nd5. There could hardly be a greater contrast with the previous game, in which White could only watch as Black methodically prepared and then carried out a kingside attack.

9 Ba3!?

A great strategist like Karpov is never going to allow Black to play
...e7-e5 for free. A so-called hacker who lives from one tactical crisis to
another could never understand why White puts his bishop on a
square where it aims at the d6-pawn, which is stoutly defended by its
fellows on c7 and e7; but if now 9...e5 then 10 dxe5, and Black cannot
recapture with 10...dxe5? without dropping the exchange. In fact he
can still avoid disaster with 10...Ng4! **(Diagram 7)**.

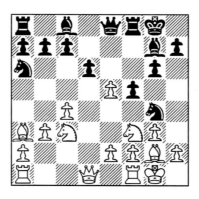

Diagram 7 (W)
Black saves himself

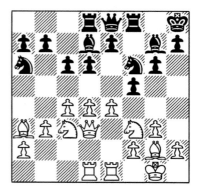

Diagram 8 (B)
Methodical play

This is an important idea in the Leningrad once White has played b2-
b3. Black has responded with a counter pin, as 11 exd6? allows
11...Bxc3. However, White can be satisfied that after say 11 Qd2 Nxe5
12 Rad1 he may not have won a pawn, but the advance ...e7-e5, the
rapier thrust of the black position, has missed its mark, leaving him
with a small but definite positional edge in a quiet position.

9...c6 10 Qd3 Bd7 11 Rfe1 Rd8 12 Rad1 Kh8 13 e4 (Diagram 8)

Wonderfully methodical play by White: he has centralised all his
pieces, or put them on squares where they influence the centre, and
now carries out the thematic advance.

13...fxe4

After 13...f4 it would be a grave mistake for White to play 14 gxf4?
when after 14...Nh5! Black threatens to take on f4 with strong counterplay. But 14 e5! would be crushing.

14 Nxe4

The lack of space in the black camp is evident from the fact that
White now threatens 15 Nxd6, checkmating the black queen!

14...Bf5

It is of some consolation to Black that at least this bishop has gained its freedom now that the barrier on f5 has vanished.

15 Nxf6 Bxf6 16 Qe3

Now Karpov makes some quiet, useful moves – he is both probing and waiting to see if Black self-destructs under the pressure.

16...Qf7 17 h3 Nc7 18 Re2 Bc8 19 Ng5 Qg8 20 Qd2 Ne6?

Here 20...h6 21 Ne4 Bg7 would win more space for his pieces. Despite all our misgivings about Black's lack of space and counterplay, he has all his pieces well entrenched and working together. The compromised Leningrad pawn structure is resilient under stress, and as long as Black holds onto the linchpin on e7, he can hope to tough things out. The game move lets White blast through this barrier.

21 Nxe6 Bxe6 22 Rde1 Bd7 23 Rxe7! (Diagram 9)

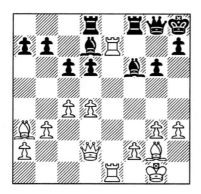

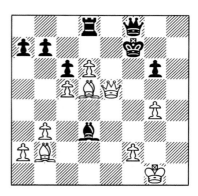

Diagram 9 (B)
White crashes through

Diagram 10 (B)
A nice finish

A rook on the seventh rank, the destruction of the base of the black pawn chain, and the removal of Black's vital dark-squared bishop – White gets all this for a small sacrifice of material.

23...Bxe7 24 Rxe7 Rf6 25 d5!

The white bishop that has waited unobtrusively on a3 since move nine suddenly becomes the star of the show. Black has no way to shore up the long dark-squared diagonal pointing at his king.

WARNING: The bishop on g7 is as vital a piece in the Leningrad Dutch as it is in the King's Indian or the Sicilian Dragon. Look after it well!

25...Qf8 26 Re3 Kg8 27 Bb2 Rf5 28 Qd4 Re5 29 Rxe5 dxe5 30 Qxe5 Kf7 31 d6 Bf5 32 c5 h5 33 g4!

I don't believe Karpov calculated 17 moves ahead when he played 17 h3, but the little pawn move certainly proves useful.

33...hxg4 34 hxg4 Bd3

Or 34...Bxg4 35 Qf6+ Kg8 36 Qxg6+ and White mates.

35 Bd5+! 1-0 (Diagram 10)

A neat finish. If 35...cxd5 then 36 Qxd5+ Ke8 37 Qe6+ and White mates.

This is a beautiful game by one of the all time greats of chess, but it is also a little depressing for fans of the Leningrad Dutch. Is it time to turn to the Classical Chapter in despair?

Before we do so, it's only right that having seen one world champion hammer the Leningrad, we give another world champion the chance to defend it.

Black's queenside counterplay: Kramnik to the Rescue

We should return to the position after 10 Qd3 in the game above **(Diagram 11)**.

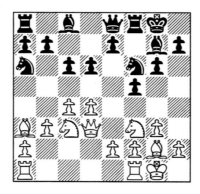

Diagram 11 (B)
Needing a concrete plan

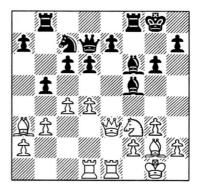

Diagram 12 (B)
Black is fine

Black made do with the straightforward developing moves 10...Bd7 and 11...Rd8 and then waited with 12...Kh8, *but the position demanded a concrete plan*. When Vladimir Kramnik was confronted with the same position as Black he started immediate, purposeful queenside action with 10...Rb8!. There followed 11 e4 fxe4 12 Nxe4 Bf5 (you will notice that compared to the Karpov game, the bishop goes to f5 in one move, rather than two – a clear saving of a tempo) 13 Nxf6+ Bxf6 14 Qe3 b5! 15 Rac1 Nc7 16 Rfe1 Qd7 17 Rcd1 **(Diagram 12)**.

So far this is Miles-Kramnik, Moscow 1989, and now according to Kramnik 17...Qc8!, intending ...Qa6 with a double attack on a3 and c4, would give Black the better chances.

You will see that Black's plan has added a lot more dynamism to the position: In the previous game it was solely a question of White pressing and Black defending, but here White has to worry about his queenside fragmenting.

Therefore, we can conclude that Black achieves lively counterplay on the queenside if White plays an early b2-b3 and aims for a quick e2-e4. Alternatively, you could enter the theoretical debate with 8...e5 as described in the notes to Game 36. For this reason, in the Leningrad main line White normally takes the opportunity to play d4-d5.

White's Central Clamp Down: 7...Qe8 8 d5

1 d4 f5 2 g3 Nf6 3 Bg2 g6 4 Nf3 Bg7 5 0-0 0-0 6 c4 d6 7 Nc3 Qe8 8 d5 (Diagram 13)

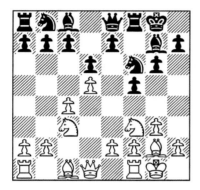

Diagram 13 (B)	**Diagram 14 (W)**
Taking action against ...e7-e5	A typical position

You may be wondering why 8 d5 is a strong move. After all, it closes the diagonal of White's own bishop on g2 and opens the a1-h8 line for the enemy bishop on g7. In fact, it is a continuation of the pawn structure warfare above: White is taking immediate action against the freeing ...e7-e5 move.

What a brilliant opening the Leningrad Dutch would be if the en passant rule had never been invented. Here, for example, Black could happily play 8...e5, knowing that he had equalised and could look forward to chances against the white king. Alas, 9 dxe6 then cuts his centre down to size, and leaves the d6-pawn vulnerable if Black moves his c-pawn. Incidentally, one of the good things about the Classical Dutch is that after d4-d5 Black can respond ...e6-e5: the pawn goes to e5 in two goes, thus nullifying the en passant rule.

Here Black has three main responses to 8 d5, depending on his seventh move. We'll start by looking at a popular line which runs 8 d5 Na6 9 Rb1 (having fixed the centre, White plans a quick queenside expansion with b2-b4) 9...c5 10 dxc6 bxc6 11 b4 Bd7 **(Diagram 14)**.

Note that Black often plays 9...c6 in this sequence, which usually amounts to the same thing after 10 dxc6 bxc6.

In order to overcome the barrier to his queenside advance on c5, White has chosen to relinquish his grip on the e6-square with 10 dxc6, whereupon the black pawn centre has regained its potential to become dynamic after ...e7-e5. Not that ...e7-e5 is automatically a good move, as it will leave the pawn on d6 backward; but Black can certainly be pleased to have it back in his armoury.

On the other hand, Black has taken a tactical risk in opening the h1-a8 diagonal, as the pawn on c6 will only provide a fragile barrier between the white bishop on g2 and the black rook on a8; moreover, White is well placed to attack the c6-pawn with gain of time by b4-b5, as the black knight will be hanging on a6. The final consideration is that Black may have an impressive centre, but after b4-b5 White has a queenside pawn majority which could yield a passed pawn – according to circumstances this passed pawn could be a weakling or a serious threat.

The position is therefore very finely balanced. The player who knows the most about the position and has the greater skill in handling it will come out on top. A possible line is 12 b5 cxb5 13 cxb5 Nc5 14 a4 Rc8 15 Nd4 Nfe4! (reducing the activity of the white bishop on g2) 16 Nxe4 Nxe4 17 Bb2 Qf7 18 e3 Qa2!? with unclear play in Alterman-Zhang Zhong, Beijing 1997.

Game 37
☐ **M.Hebden** ■ **N.Firman**
Lausanne 2000

1 d4 f5 2 g3 Nf6 3 Bg2 g6 4 Nf3 Bg7 5 0-0 0-0 6 c4 d6 7 Nc3 Qe8 8 d5

Another way to get a pawn on d5 is with 8 Nd5!?, which tries to take advantage of Black's queen move by hitting c7. Then after 8...Nxd5 9 cxd5 White has nobbled the black centre and as a bonus has potential pressure down the c-file. However, the advanced pawn on d5 is far easier to eliminate here than after 8 d5, for example 9...Nd7!? (or 9...c6!? immediately) 10 Ng5 (trying to take advantage of the hole on e6) 10...Nb6 11 a4 c6! 12 dxc6 bxc6 13 d5 c5 14 Qc2 Rb8 with unclear play.

8...Na6

Alternatively Black could spend a move opposing White's queenside advance with 8...a5!?.

9 Rb1 c5 10 dxc6 bxc6 11 b4 Bd7 12 a3

White decides to dig in on the queenside rather than press forwards at once with 12 b5, which has been discussed above.

12...h6

As White is undertaking nothing active on the queenside, Black uses the breathing space to advance his kingside pawns and set up a future attack.

13 Bb2 g5! (Diagram 15)

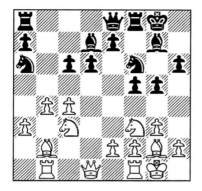

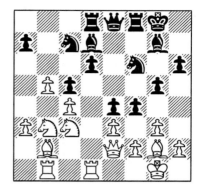

Diagram 15 (W)
Expanding on the kingside

Diagram 16 (W)
A direct attack

Here very natural was 13...Qf7, putting the queen in a handy gap in Black's pawn structure and attacking c4. Alas, this fails to 14 c5! giving Black a very ugly choice between 14...d5? 15 Ne5, 14...dxc5 15 Ne5 Qe8 16 b5 when 16...cxb5 17 Bxa8 Qxa8 would be a good exchange sacrifice if 18 Nxd7 didn't then win a piece, and 14...Ne8 (best, as it at least keeps a hold on the e5-square) 15 cxd6 exd6, and the black centre is much compromised.

WARNING: Always be on the lookout for pawn moves that smash up your centre.

14 e3?!

Still hoping for 14...Qf7 15 c5! but this slow move does nothing to disturb his opponent. White is hoping to keep a solid positional edge, but time isn't really on his side as in the long term the broad black centre is going to come up trumps.

There were two active approaches possible. Firstly, 14 Qd3 threatens 15 c5, exposing an attack on the knight on a6. Then 14...Nc7 15 b5 reverts to queenside action after all. Or secondly, 14 c5!? (anyway!) 14...g4!? (to stop the white knight going to e5) 15 Nh4 dxc5 looks unclear.

14...Nc7 15 Qe2

The white queen moves to a passive square. Instead 15 Qd3, keeping an eye on d6, would at least prevent Black's next move.

15...e5!

A courageous and correct decision: Black has judged that the attacking energy generated by this advance will outweigh the static weakness created on d6.

16 Rfd1 e4 17 Nd4

The knight jumps to a central post, but on the other hand it gets in the way of an attack on d6.

17...Rd8 18 b5?

Here this long awaited advance is positively harmful as it allows Black to drive the white knight from d4.

18...c5 19 Nb3 f4! (Diagram 16)

With the knights away on the queenside and a rook no longer on f1, the white kingside is seriously under-defended. This permits Black to launch a direct attack.

20 exf4 Bg4 21 f3 exf3 22 Bxf3 Qh5

A computer might be happy to be a pawn up here, but few humans relish facing an all-out assault in which one slip can be fatal.

23 Nd2 Rde8 24 Qg2 Bxf3 25 Nxf3 Ng4!

The knight's entry on e3 causes havoc, as if 26 Qe2 then 26...Nf5 wins at least a piece as the white queen needs to keep f3 defended.

26 Rxd6 Ne3 27 Qf2 Nxc4 28 Nd5?

The only chance was 28 Rd7, though 28...Ne6 keeps up the pressure.

28...Nxd5 29 Bxg7

If 29 Rxd5 Nxb2 wins – again the main problem is that the white queen is tied down to the defence of the knight on f3. Therefore, White ends up a piece down.

29...Nxd6 30 Bxf8 Ne4 31 Qg2 Kxf8 32 g4 Qg6 33 Ne5 Qh7 34 Re1 Ndf6 35 Qf3 gxf4 36 Qxf4 Kg8 37 a4 Qc7 38 Nd3 Qxf4 39 Nxf4 Nxg4 40 a5 Ngf6 41 Kg2 Rb8 42 Rb1 Nc3 43 Rc1 Nfe4 0-1

Black's kingside pawn advances worked well in this game, but remember this isn't always the correct strategy. Every position has to be judged on its own merits. Here as a warning is an example in which the same pawn advance ...e7-e5 proved a disaster.

Game 38
☐ **B.Larsen** ■ **J.Tisdall**
London 1990

---

1 c4 f5 2 Nc3 Nf6 3 d4 g6 4 g3 Bg7 5 Bg2 0-0 6 Nf3 d6 7 0-0 Nc6 8 d5 Na5 9 Qa4 c5 10 dxc6 bxc6 11 Nd4 c5 12 Ndb5 Rb8 13 Nxa7 Bd7 14 Nab5 Kh8 15 Bg5 h6 16 Bxf6 Bxf6 17 Rac1 Bxc3 18 Rxc3 Nxc4 19 Qxc4 Bxb5 20 Qf4 Kg7 21 Qe3 (Diagram 17)

Black has an impressive-looking pawn centre, which he decided to utilise at once with...

21...e5?.

Compared to the Firman game above, there are very few pieces on the board. This means that Black is short of resources either to defend his pawn centre or carry out an attack. Indeed, how can an attack possibly hope to succeed? The white king is better defended than the black king, with both a tighter pawn cover and a bishop on g2 to shelter behind.

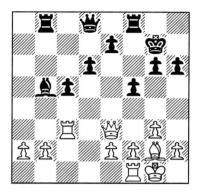

Diagram 17 (B)
Is it time for central activity?

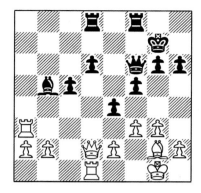

Diagram 18 (B)
Opening a second front

Therefore, as it is inadequately supported by pieces and there are no targets in the white camp, the ...e7-e5 advance does nothing dynamic – which means it is just leaving a backward pawn on d6 and making the black king less safe. The game continued

22 Rd1 Qf6 23 Qd2

The white pieces besiege the d6 pawn from the front...

23...Rbd8 24 Ra3!

...and prepare to attack it from the side with Ra6 after driving the black bishop away.

24...e4

Black would like to get his bishop to e6 and then play ...d6-d5, but this fails after 24...Bc4 25 b3 Be6 26 Ra6 d5 27 Bxd5! Rxd5 28 Qxd5 Bxd5 29 Rxf6 Kxf6 30 Rxd5 and White is a pawn up in the rook and pawn endgame. Therefore he tries to shut in the white bishop first before carrying out the manoeuvre.

25 f3! (Diagram 18)

Opening a second front, as if immediately 25 Ra5 then 25...Bc4 26 b3 Be6 27 Ra6 d5 consolidates the black centre.

25...exf3 26 Bxf3 Rd7

It is too late for 26...Bc4 as then 27 b3 Be6 28 Ra6 d5 29 Qe3! (even better than 29 Bxd5) attacks both c5 and e6.

27 b4! Rff7

The black bishop runs out of squares after 27...cxb4 28 Qxb4 or 27...c4 28 Qd5!.

28 Ra5 Bc4 29 bxc5 1-0

Black Plays 7...c6 8 d5 e5 9 dxe6 Bxe6

In this variation Black takes the bull by the horns and forces an immediate clarification in the centre.

1 d4 f5 2 g3 Nf6 3 Bg2 g6 4 Nf3 Bg7 5 0-0 0-0 6 c4 d6 7 Nc3 c6 8 d5 e5 9 dxe6 Bxe6 (Diagram 19)

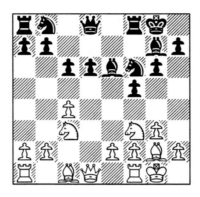

Diagram 19 (W)	**Diagram 20 (B)**
Not so bad!	Defending c4

Before you get up in arms about the disgusting weakness left on d6, consider the following:

1) Black's light-squared bishop often spends a long time shut in behind the pawn structure in the Leningrad. Here it can already see daylight and is actually attacking something: the white pawn on c4.

2) The black queen has acquired a nice square on e7, where she clears the way for the black rook on a8 to enter the game via d8.

3) White's pawn spearhead on d5 has vanished, which has taken the pressure off the c6-pawn: White no longer has ideas of d5xc6 followed, after the recapture ...b7xc6, by a queenside advance based on Rb1 with b4-b5. Therefore the black queenside is on the whole more secure than in the 7...Qe8 variation, which means White's bishop on g2 is in danger of spending the middlegame staring at a brick wall on c6.

Of course, we cannot ignore the backward pawn on d6, which is undoubtedly a serious structural weakness. It sits on an open file, which means it can be attacked from the front by the white queen and rooks; it can also be assaulted diagonally with Bf4. Still, it isn't so easy for White to get at the pawn as he also has to think about the defence of his own pawn on c4. Furthermore, Black can achieve a rapid, compact development, and there are lots of pieces at hand to aid the defence of d6.

So there is a lot to be said in favour of the immediate breakout with 8...e5. However, I don't recommend you play like this as Black for one reason: the variation is terribly dull! Black gets to centralise his pieces and there is little danger of d6 dropping off if he is vigilant: but then what? There is no way to inject counterattacking energy into the black set-up, unless White goes seriously wrong. I have played this variation several times as Black and I find that I get the urge to do something active and merely end up weakening myself on the queenside or kingside. You will need a lot of patience to play this variation – and even then you are unlikely to get more than a draw.

Game 39
□ **E.Vovsha** ■ **V.Malaniuk**
Linz 1997

---

1 Nf3 f5 2 d4 g6 3 g3 Bg7 4 Bg2 Nf6 5 0-0 0-0 6 c4 d6 7 Nc3 c6 8 d5 e5 9 dxe6 Bxe6 10 Qd3 (Diagram 20)

White defends c4 and at the same time clears the way for Rd1 to attack the d6-pawn. If White plays 10 b3, then 10...Ne4? isn't recommended, as after 11 Nxe4 Bxa1 12 Nxd6 White has a superb initiative and besides will easily gain two pawns for the exchange. Instead 10...Na6 would be a solid response with play similar to the game. Note that 11 Bf4? would then be a bad idea because of the standard trick 11...Nh5! 12 Bxd6?? Bxc3.

10...Re8

Hereabouts Black's thoughts are dominated by one question: how do I generate enough counterplay against c4 to prevent White winning the d6-pawn in a 'clean' manner?

Also reasonable is 10...Nbd7, as 11 Qxd6 Bxc4 offers White nothing while 11 Bf4 Nb6! 12 b3 (or 12 Bxd6 Bxc4) 12...Ne4 gives Black enough activity. A sharper alternative is 10...Na6, when if 11 Bf4 Black should offer a pawn sacrifice rather than become tied down to the defence of d6: 11...Ne4! 12 Nxe4 fxe4 13 Qxe4 Nc5! and White has no way to consolidate his ill gotten gains, for example 14 Qc2 (or 14 Qe3 Bxc4) 14...Bf5 15 Qd1 Qb6! 16 Bxd6 Rfd8 17 Bxc5 Rxd1 18 Bxb6 Rxa1 19 Rxa1 axb6 when Black's huge pressure on the queenside is sure to recoup his material with ...Bxb2 etc. and it is White who will be struggling to draw. Instead White could play slightly more modestly with 11 Ng5 Qe7 12 Bf4 Rad8 13 Rad1 though here also Black can push him back with 13...Nh5! as if 14 Bxd6? Qxg5. We can see from the above lines that White doesn't have the power to capture the d6-pawn with the straightforward Bf4 without encountering serious problems elsewhere.

11 Ng5

Black's previous move set a nice trap: if 11 Bf4 Ne4! 12 Nxe4?? fxe4 13 Qxe4 then 13...Bf5! and the white queen is trapped in the centre of the board.

Meanwhile after 11 b3 Black can activate his game with 11...Ne4! 12

Bb2 Na6 13 Qc2 d5! with unclear play.

11...Nbd7 12 Nxe6 Rxe6 (Diagram 21)

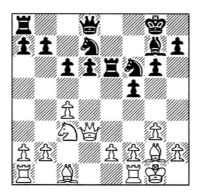

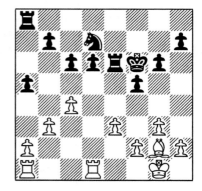

Diagram 21 (W)
A favourable exchange?

Diagram 22 (W)
A good ending for Black

You might imagine that the exchange of knight for bishop has been of more profit to White than Black. In fact this is by no means certain. If White had managed somehow to exchange his knight for the bishop on g7, it would have been an undoubted positional triumph, as all the dark squares around the black king would have been left sickly. However, here it Black's light-squared bishop that has been exchanged, a piece which is very much the poor cousin of the bishop on g7.

Not only was the bishop on e6 hampered by Black's own light-squared pawn chain, but it was also cluttering up the black position. Usually Black gets his queen's rook to d8 and then sticks the bishop back on c8, where it is inactive but at least doesn't get in the way – and of course is ready to spring to life if White breaks open the position.

After the exchange, White's bishop on g2 is rid of its direct rival for control of the light squares, but it is hard to see how it has benefited: the d5-square is unavailable and Black has a firmer hold on e4 than before the exchange.

So, all in all, can it really be said that the black bishop on e6 was of more value than the white knight?

13 Qc2 Qe7 14 e3

If this is White's best move then he can't claim to have kept any opening advantage. Evidently he should have tried the double-edged line with 11 b3 as given above.

14...a5!

Black fixes White's queenside pawns as a prelude to attacking them.

15 b3 Ne4 16 Bb2 Nxc3 17 Bxc3 Bxc3 18 Qxc3 Qg7 19 Qxg7+?

A bad strategical mistake. The endgame is better for Black, so White should have kept the queens on the board with say 19 Qd2. Then if Black pressed too hard for the win on the queenside his king might end up a target.

19...Kxg7 20 Rfd1 Kf6 (Diagram 22)

The following strategical factors determine Black's advantage: firstly, the d6-pawn can be easily defended by the black king if necessary, so it can no longer be considered a weakness; secondly, the white bishop on g2 has far less scope than the black knight, which has a lovely square on c5; and thirdly, the white queenside can be put under pressure with an attacking plan based on ...a5-a4 – given time Black might play ...Nc5, ...Ra6, ...Rb6 and ...Rb4 as necessary to prevent the reply b3-b4, and then ...a5-a4, when White's pawn structure collapses. It will be seen from all this that White is weak on the dark squares.

21 e4!?

Rather than await Black's gradual build up the queenside White uses tactics to activate his bishop, but Malaniuk is ready with a fine positional exchange sacrifice.

21...fxe4! 22 Bh3 Ne5 23 Bxe6 Kxe6 24 Kg2 d5 25 cxd5+ cxd5

The king and knight excellently support Black's pawn centre. For the moment Black has to concentrate on preventing White from breaking things up with f2-f3 or activating his rooks.

26 Rac1 Kd6!

Here for example he has stop White playing 27 Rc7.

27 Rc2 Rf8 28 Rcd2 Nd3 (Diagram 23)

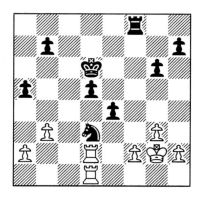

Diagram 23 (W)
A powerful knight

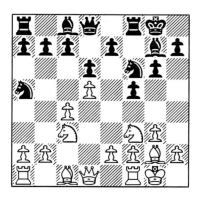

Diagram 24 (W)
Attacking c4

Now Black is threatening to increase the pressure by bringing his king all the way down to c3. White tries to escape by giving back the material, but Black's passed pawn and more active king allow him to squeeze out the win. Objectively speaking, White should have continued to wait, which would put the onus on Black to find a winning path. However, it's not at all easy to defend passively with no hope of counterplay – unless of course you happen to be a computer.

29 Rxd3? exd3 30 Rxd3 Rf7 31 Rd2 Ke5 32 Re2+ Kd4 33 Rd2+ Ke4 34 Kf1 d4 35 Re2+ Kd3 36 Ke1 Rc7 37 Rd2+ Kc3 38 Kd1 d3 39 f4 Kd4 40 Rb2 Ke3 41 Rd2 h5 42 Rb2 Rc3 43 Rd2 Kf3 0-1

White resigned as if 44 Rb2 then 44...Rc2! 45 Rxc2 dxc2+ 46 Kxc2 Kg2 and the black king captures on h2 and g3.

Black Plays 7...Nc6

The move 7...Nc6 has been unjustly ignored by Dutch theorists. It intends to establish the ideal pawn centre with 8...e5, and so White has little choice but to play 8 d5, whereupon Black has a key decision to make: should the knight on c6 go to the queenside or to the centre? We'll consider both 8...Na5 and 8...Ne5.

The Line 8 d5 Na5

1 d4 f5 2 g3 Nf6 3 Bg2 g6 4 Nf3 Bg7 5 0-0 0-0 6 c4 d6 7 Nc3 Nc6 8 d5 Na5 (Diagram 24)

Here the knight attacks the c4-pawn, but once White deals with the threat it will be a case of the hunter hunted, as there will be a threat of b2-b4, trapping the poor beast. Therefore, the advance ...c7-c5 will be essential to safeguard the knight.

After 9 Nd2 c5, White has two main moves:

Firstly, 10 a3 is well met by the nonchalant 10...Bd7! when if 11 b4, apparently winning the knight, Black has the tactical response 11...cxb4 12 axb4 Nxc4! 13 Nxc4 Qc7 14 Qb3 Rfc8 when he will regain the piece with a good game thanks to the pin on the c-file. So White should play more reservedly with 11 Qc2 which defends his own knight on c3 as a prelude to a fianchetto: 11...Qc7 12 b3 (White reinforces his hold on c4 in anticipation of an attack with ...b7-b5) 12...a6 13 Bb2 Rab8 14 Nd1 b5 (Black has carried out his planned advance) 15 Bc3! (the bishop sidesteps any tactical tricks based on ...Rxb2! as the b-file is about to be opened; it also ties down the black queen to defending a5) 15...bxc4 16 bxc4 Rb7! 17 Rb1 Rfb8 **(Diagram 25)**.

We have reached an interesting middlegame position. The black knight on a5 is paralysed, but it hasn't become an outcast from the other black pieces: it is contributing to the plan of queenside action by putting pressure on c4. Black will look for an opportune moment to offer an exchange of dark-squared bishops in order to increase his chances down the b-file. One game continued from here 18 Rxb7 Rxb7 19 Nb2 Qb8! 20 e3 Nb3 21 Nf3 Ne4! with a good position for Black.

The alternative is 10 Qc2. As there is no immediate threat of trapping the black knight, Black can afford to play in the centre if he chooses with 10...e5!?. Here is an example of Black's tactical chances after this advance.

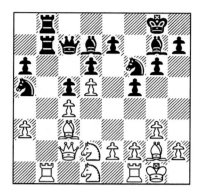

Diagram 25 (B)
An interesting middlegame

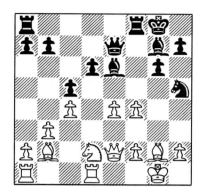

Diagram 26 (W)
Hitting f4

Game 40
☐ **J.Piket** ■ **M.Gurevich**
Lucerne 1989

1 d4 f5 2 Nf3 Nf6 3 c4 g6 4 g3 Bg7 5 Bg2 0-0 6 0-0 d6 7 Nc3 Nc6 8 d5 Na5 9 Qc2

A sneaky move order that cuts no ice with Gurevich.

9...c5!

Black has no wish to open the c-file: if 9...Nxc4? 10 Nb5 a6?! 11 Nbd4! Nb6 12 Ng5 the invasion on e6 is well worth a pawn. Therefore he leads play back to the main line.

10 Nd2 e5 11 dxe6 Bxe6 12 Rd1 Qe7 13 b3 Nc6 14 Bb2 Nd4 15 Qd3?

The queen had to hide away on c1 as here she becomes vulnerable to tactics.

15...f4! 16 gxf4 Bf5! 17 e4 Be6

The bishop provoked White's last move so that f4 can no longer be protected by e2-e3.

18 Ne2 Nxe2+ 19 Qxe2 Nh5! (Diagram 26)

By now you should be familiar with the idea of a temporary pawn sacrifice that aims to open up f4 for the knight

20 Nf1 Nxf4 21 Qc2 Bxb2 22 Qxb2 Bh3! 23 Bf3 Bxf1 24 Kxf1 Qh4 0-1

One finish is 24...Qh4 25 Kg1 Nh3+ 26 Kg2 Qg5+ 27 Kxh3 Rxf3 mate.

Instead of 9 Nd2, White can attack the knight immediately with his queen with 9 Qa4!?. This is probably the critical move as it has featured in some high level Dutch games. Then 9...c5 10 dxc6 bxc6 11 c5! **(Diagram 27)** breaks up Black's centre.

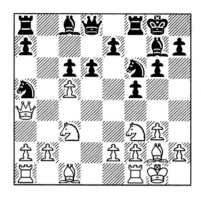

Diagram 27 (B)
Breaking up the centre

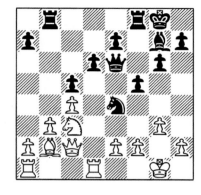

Diagram 28 (B)
A surprising decision

Now 11...d5? 12 Ne5 looks very awkward, but fortunately 11...dxc5! is by no means as bad as it looks as Black can utilise the b-file for counterplay. Here are two examples: 12 Ne5 Rb8 13 Nc4 Rb4! 14 Qxa5 Rxc4 15 Qxa7 Nd5 16 Bd2 f4! (Haba-Agdestein, Cappelle La Grande 2000); and 13 Rd1 Qb6 14 Be3 Ng4! 15 Nc4 Nxc4 16 Qxc4+ Kh8 17 Bxc5 Ba6! 18 Bxb6 Bxc4 19 Bxa7 Rxb2 (Erdos-Kun, Savaria 2002). In both cases Black has an initiative that outweighs the defects in his pawn structure.

Game 41
☐ **L.Spassov** ■ **M.Marin**
Berga 1993

1 Nf3 f5 2 g3 Nf6 3 Bg2 g6 4 0-0 Bg7 5 d4 0-0 6 c4 d6 7 Nc3 Nc6 8 d5 Na5 9 Qa4 c5 10 dxc6 bxc6 11 Nd4

White ducks the challenge of the complex variations after 11 c5.

11...Bd7!? 12 Rd1

After 12 Nxc6 Nxc6 13 Bxc6 Bxc6 14 Qxc6 Rc8 15 Qa4 Qd7! White temporarily has an extra pawn but it is difficult to see how he can hold onto c4 as b2-b3 will always lead to disaster after Black's ...Ne4 riposte. Still, White should have tested this line, as he now gradually drifts into a prospectless position.

12...c5 13 Nc6 Nxc6 14 Bxc6 Rb8 15 Bxd7 Qxd7 16 Qc2 Qe6 17 b3 Ne4 18 Bb2 (Diagram 28)

What follows is a perfect illustration of the role of the initiative in the mainline Dutch.

White is solidly entrenched in the centre and on the queenside, but his king is lacking in defenders – in fact every white piece has moved away from the kingside. In particular the king's bishop, always the staunchest defender of the white king, is missing from g2. This indicates that there are potential weaknesses on light squares such as f3, g2 and h3. Already Black has exploited this light square malaise to put his knight on e4.

White would like to diminish the force of Black's coming attack by exchanging off both minor pieces with Nxe4 and then Bxg7. In that case Black would still undoubtedly have the initiative, thanks to the f-file after ...f5xe4, which he could use to pressurise the f2-square with his rooks; but White would have got off relatively lightly.

Instead Black gave up his Indian bishop with

18...Bxc3!

If White had the initiative this would be a disastrous decision, as the long dark-squared diagonal leading to the black king is left bereft of defence. Here, however, it is Black who has the initiative, which amounts to the right to attack. The exchange on c3 has eliminated the only white minor piece able to fight for control of the light squares. Black's own knight is therefore free to take part in a plan of attack aimed at exploiting the holes in the white kingside.

As Black dictates events on the kingside, the absence of a bishop on g2 is more significant than the missing black bishop on g7.

18...Bxc3 19 Bxc3 f4 20 Be1 f3! (Diagram 29)

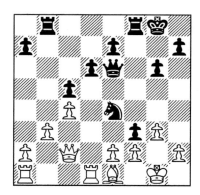

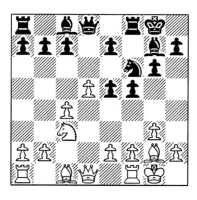

Diagram 29 (W)	Diagram 30 (W)
Feasting on the light squares	A change in structure

Black makes himself master over all the light squares around the white king.

21 exf3 Rxf3 22 Rd3 Ng5 23 h4 Nh3+ 24 Kf1 Qe4 25 Rad1 Rxg3!
26 fxg3 Qh1+ 27 Ke2 Qg2+ 0-1

White loses his queen.

The Line 7...Nc6 8 d5 Ne5 9 Nxe5 dxe5

1 d4 f5 2 g3 Nf6 3 Bg2 g6 4 Nf3 Bg7 5 0-0 0-0 6 c4 d6 7 Nc3 Nc6 8 d5 Ne5 9 Nxe5 dxe5 (Diagram 30)

Black has achieved a mobile pawn centre of the type that White's 8 d5 was specifically designed to prevent. It is true that the cost has been high: Black's queenside pawn structure has been seriously damaged in the process. Therefore, the crucial question is whether Black can generate enough counterplay on the kingside before the darkness sets in on the other wing. This is a hugely complex and exciting variation, involving heavy sacrifices and sudden attacks. Whether or not it is theoretically sound, it is terrifying for the white king!

Game 42
☐ **A.Kremenietsky** ■ **T.Rendle**
Chekhov 2000

---

1 d4 f5 2 c4 Nf6 3 Nc3 d6 4 Nf3 g6 5 g3 Bg7 6 Bg2 0-0 7 0-0 Nc6 8 d5 Ne5 9 Nxe5 dxe5 10 e4

One of the two main responses. It is designed to disrupt Black in the centre – or at least it should do if White plays it right!

10...f4 11 b4??

A natural move, but here it is a disastrous strategical mistake. If you know why, then congratulations: you really do understand the Dutch! If not, then let me console you by pointing out that the young Anatoly Karpov made the identical error – he was crushed as well.

If Black can bypass the pawn on e4 with ...f5-f4 and at the same time keep the centre blocked, he has the makings of a strong attack. Therefore, the one and only way to justify White's previous move was with 11 gxf4, with a vigorous struggle in prospect. The theory goes 11...exf4 (instead 11... Nh5 12 fxe5 Bxe5 13 Ne2 Qd6 14 f4! – as usual in this variation Black mustn't be allowed to stabilise his control of the centre – 14...Nxf4 15 Bxf4 Bxf4 16 Nxf4 Rxf4 17 Rxf4 Qxf4 18 Qd4 is given in various sources as good for White, but 18...Qg5 is by no means clear) 12 e5 (here 12 Bxf4? Nxe4 13 Nxe4 Rxf4 is a very favourable exchange for Black as he gets rid of White's strong bishop) 12...Ng4 13 e6 (White's pawn structure looks crushing, but Black can break it up) 13...Ne5 14 Re1 Nxc4 15 Re4 Nd6 16 Rxf4 c6! with unclear play in Gordon-Rendle, Scarborough 2004.

11...g5! (Diagram 31)

If now 11 gxf4 the reply 11...gxf4 keeps the centre blocked and sets Black up nicely for an assault down the g-file. Therefore, White has no means of distracting Black from a direct attack on the kingside, as his own counterplay on the queenside is painfully ineffective.

12 Bb2 Qe8!

Black could have prepared this with 12...a6, but there is no reason to be afraid of White's next move.

13 Nb5 Ng4! 14 h3

After 14 Nxc7 Qh5 it is soon all over: 15 h3 f3! 16 hxg4 Bxg4 17 Bh1 Rf6 and mate quickly follows on the h-file after 18...Rh6.

14...Qh5! 15 hxg4 Bxg4 16 f3

Mate follows as in the note above after 16 Qd3 f3 intending ...Rf6, etc.

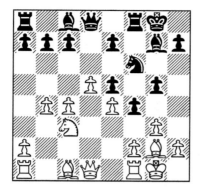

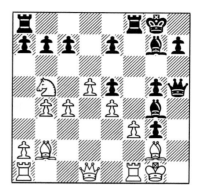

Diagram 31 (W)
Attack on the kingside

Diagram 32 (W)
Black is winning

16...fxg3 (Diagram 32) 17 Rf2

The threat of mate on h2 forces White to accept huge material losses, as 17 Re1 Qh2+ 18 Kf1 Rxf3+ 19 Qxf3 Bxf3 20 Bxf3 Qf2 is mate. The rest is just a carve-up.

TIP: Remember this common mating pattern with a black pawn on g3 and a queen on h2.

17...Qh2+ 18 Kf1 gxf2 19 fxg4 Qg1+ 20 Ke2 Qxg2 21 Qf1 Qxg4+ 22 Ke3 Qf4+ 23 Kd3 Qf3+ 24 Kd2 g4 25 Nc3 Bh6+ 26 Kc2 g3 27 Nd1 Qxe4+ 28 Kc3 Qe1+ 0-1

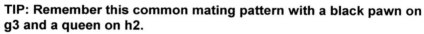

Game 43
☐ **H.Erdogan** ■ **P.Varley**
European Team Championship, Leon 2001

1 d4 d6

Yet another way of reaching the Dutch to add to our collection. Of course, Black must be ready for the Pirc or Modern after 2 e4.

2 Nf3 g6 3 c4 Bg7 4 Nc3 f5 5 g3 Nf6 6 Bg2 0-0 7 0-0 Nc6 8 d5 Ne5 9 Nxe5 dxe5 10 e4 Nd7!?

An interesting retreat. Black wants to be able to advance ...f5-f4 without giving White the chance to break in the centre as occurs after 10...f4 11 gxf4 exf4 12 e5 – see the note to White's 11th move in the previous game. The knight also performs a useful role in stopping c4-c5. Still, it is a paradoxical move. Black moves his knight away from the kingside in order to ...start an attack on the kingside!

11 exf5

As usual in the 9...dxe5 variation, White is feeling a little confused by the unexpected turn of events. The pawn structure is nothing like he imagined it would be when he played 8 d5, and he has trouble adjusting to the new situation. The energetic 11 f4 appears to be the correct way to meet Black's slow knight move, for example 11...fxe4 12 Nxe4 exf4 13 Bxf4 Bxb2 14 Rb1 Bg7 15 c5 with a lot of pressure for the pawn.

11...gxf5 12 f4 e4 13 Be3? (Diagram 33)

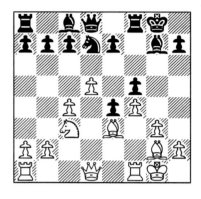 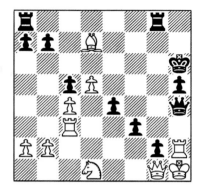

Diagram 33 (B)
Too passive

Diagram 34 (W)
Day of the pawns

Again this is too passive. White has to strike quickly for if Black is allowed to consolidate his pawn centre he will gain a strong initiative on the kingside. Therefore 13 g4! to undermine the e4-pawn looks right, when after 13...Nb6!? the speculative 14 c5!? Bxc3 15 bxc3 Nxd5 is double-edged – Black has a pawn more but White has a potentially powerful dark-squared bishop.

However, 14 Qb3! promises White some advantage – Black's best reply is probably 14...e6!?. In any event, it was vital for White to widen the struggle to the queenside and centre, as after the game move Black can focus undisturbed on his kingside attack.

13...Nf6 14 Qd2 Bd7 15 Rfd1 Qe8!

The black queen will be excellently placed on g6 where she will help to wear down White's defences on the g-file.

16 Bd4 Qg6 17 Bf1 h5! 18 Qg2 Ng4 19 Bxg7 Kxg7 20 Rd2 c5!

A fine move that slows down White's counterplay in the centre long enough for Black's kingside assault to reach full power.

21 Nd1 Rh8 22 h4

An ugly move, but 22...h4 had to be stopped. Now Black turns his attention to the weak pawn on g3.

22...Kh6 23 Rc1 Rhg8 24 Rc3 Qd6 25 Be2?! e5!

Black seizes the chance given to him by White's last move to rip away the white kingside pawns, as if 26 dxe6? then 26...Qxd2.

26 Bxg4 exf4!!

A piece sacrifice that releases all the potential energy of the black pawns.

27 Bh3 f3 28 Qh2 f4 29 Kh1 fxg3 30 Qg1 Qf4 31 Bxd7 Qxh4+ 32 Rh2 g2+ 0-1 (Diagram 34)

The complete triumph of the infantry!

Game 44
□ **Y.Pelletier** ■ **F.Vallejo Pons**
Biel 2002

---

1 d4 f5 2 g3 g6 3 Bg2 Bg7 4 c4 Nf6 5 Nc3 d6 6 Nf3 0-0 7 0-0 Nc6 8 d5 Ne5 9 Nxe5 dxe5 10 c5! (Diagram 35)

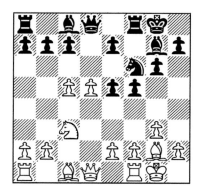

Diagram 35 (B)
The critical test

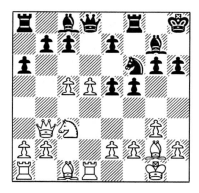

Diagram 36 (W)
Preventing Nb5

The critical test of Black's opening strategy. White intends to bludgeon his way through the queenside as quickly as possible.

10...Kh8

As it is basically a race between White's attack on the queenside and Black's on the kingside, you may be wondering why Black plays this slow-looking move rather than 10...h6 straightaway. In fact it amounts to the same thing as after 10...h6 11 Qb3 the black king will need to be evacuated with 11...Kh8 to prevent 12 d6+. Black wants to keep the centre situation as static as possible and so doesn't want to allow White to open lines there with a discovered check.

11 Qb3 h6 12 Rd1 a6! (Diagram 36)

Black intends ...Qe8 and doesn't want to be disturbed by 13 Nb5 threatening a big fork on c7 – unlike in the Rendle game above, his position isn't so powerful that he can be indifferent to the loss of a rook.

13 Bd2!

White's strongest plan involves putting this bishop on a5, where it will attack the c7-pawn.

13...Qe8 14 Rac1 g5 15 Na4 e4

Alas for Black, if 15...Qh5 then 16 Ba5 is strong. Therefore he turns to his mass of centre pawns for counterplay – and with good judgment, as White's bishop on g2 is shut out of the action.

16 Ba5 Bd7 17 Nc3 Rc8?

This move, however, is based on a misconception. Black tries to hold together his queenside using tactical means, but it was too late for such niceties. He had to mess up the position with 17...b6! (getting rid of White's strong c5-pawn) 18 cxb6 cxb6 19 Qxb6 Rb8 20 Qxa6 Rxb2. Then White has a passed pawn on a2, but it is a feeble thing compared to the monsters he gets on the b- and c-files in the game. Meanwhile Black has his large mobile clump of pawns in the centre. The word 'unclear' is made for such positions: the player who shows the most determination and inventiveness will win as either colour. Of course, this is a moral victory for Black, as his opponent always starts the game with a small but definite advantage.

18 Qxb7! Rb8

Black's idea is that he either gets to keep on attacking the white queen or he wins a bishop. This is true, but after...

19 Qxc7 Rc8 20 Qb7 Rb8 21 Qxa6 Ra8 22 Qb6 Rb8 23 Qa6 Ra8 24 Qc4! Rxa5 25 c6 (Diagram 37)

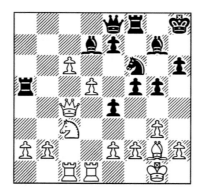 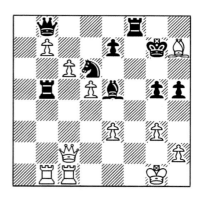

Diagram 37 (B)
Impressive pawns

Diagram 38 (B)
White is coming in

...White's phalanx of passed pawns is worth far more than a piece.

25...Bc8 26 b4 Ra8 27 b5 Qd8 28 Qc5 Ne8

Black gives up his attacking aspirations on the kingside in order to try to set up a blockade of the passed pawns. It is a sure sign that his opening strategy has failed when the knight has to go backwards.

29 b6 Nd6 30 Rb1 Ba6 31 a4 Qb8 32 Nb5 Bxb5 33 axb5 Ra2 34 b7 Be5 35 Rdc1 Ra4 36 e3 Kh7 37 Bh3 h5 38 Qc2 Ra5 3 Bf1 f4

A desperate bid for activity, but with the black queen pressed to the wall by the passed pawns it is inevitable that White will be able to use the open lines on the kingside to launch a decisive attack of his own.

40 Bg2 fxe3 41 fxe3 Kg7 42 Bxe4 Rxb5 43 Bh7! (Diagram 38)

TIP: If the main body of the opponent's pieces is tied down on one side of the board, try to attack him on the other side. Here you can't get much further away than the h-file!

43...Rxb1 44 Rxb1 Ne8 45 Qg6+ Kh8 46 Qh6?

This proves good enough, but 46 d6! was the killer move: 46...Bxd6 (46...Nxd6 47 Bg8! Rxg8 48 Qh6 mate or similarly 46...exd6 47 c7! Nxc7 48 Bg8 Rxg8 49 Qh6 mate) 47 Qh6 Rf7 48 Bf5+ Kg8 49 Be6 Ng7 50 Qg6 Qf8 51 Bxf7+ Qxf7 52 b8Q+ etc.

46...Bg7 47 Qxg5 Kxh7 48 Qxe7 Rf5 49 c7 Nxc7 50 Qe4 Kg6 51 Rf1 Qxb7 52 Qxf5+ Kh6 53 d6 Nd5 54 Qe6+ Kh7 55 Qe4+ 1-0

Chapter Eight

Leningrad Dutch: Other Ideas

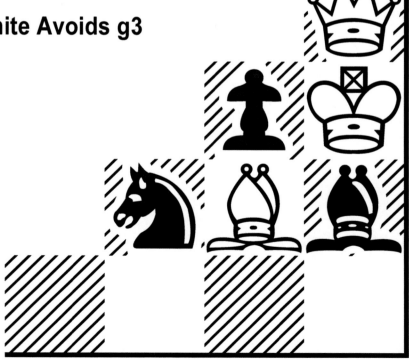

Here we shall consider divergences by White from the Leningrad main line, which was discussed in the previous chapter. There are four main ideas: Nh3 instead of Nf3; a quick grab of queenside territory with b2-b4; c2-c3 rather than c2-c4; and the avoidance of a fianchetto on g2, which includes a sharp attacking line with h2-h4.

Theoretical?

Yes: don't imagine that these are harmless sidelines played solely because White is afraid of entering the main line. They have all occurred frequently in top-class chess, so White might well be armed with some serious preparation if he adopts one of them.

White Plays Nh3

White can put his knight on h3 at any point between move four and seven. For example: 1 d4 f5 2 g3 Nf6 3 Bg2 g6 4 Nh3 **(Diagram 1)** or 1 d4 f5 2 g3 Nf6 3 Bg2 g6 4 c4 d6 5 Nc3 Bg7 6 d5 0-0 7 Nh3 **(Diagram 2)**.

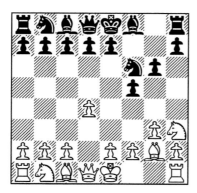

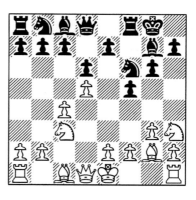

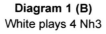
Diagram 1 (B)
White plays 4 Nh3

Diagram 2 (B)
White plays 7 Nh3

White plans a quick Nf4 and h2-h4 Attack

In combination with the pawn advance d4-d5, the wing development of the knight is a formidable response to the Leningrad. On the whole it is less powerful if Black has the capacity to play ...e6-e5 with no fear of the en passant rule. This is the case if White plays 5 Nf4, without bothering to arrange d4-d5, though Black still needs to be careful.

NOTE: Black has to watch out for a quick h4-h5 attack when the white knight goes to f4, as the g6-pawn is an attractive target.

Black's best response to 5 Nf4 will vary depending on whether he has played 4...d6 or 4...Bg7.

Thus after 1 d4 f5 2 g3 Nf6 3 Bg2 g6 4 Nh3 d6 5 Nf4 Black can play 5...c6 6 h4 e5! 7 dxe5 dxe5 8 Qxd8+ Kxd8 9 Nd3 Nbd7 10 Bg5 Be7! 11 Nd2 e4 **(Diagram 3)** and his chances already looked preferable in Eingorn-Dolmatov, Moscow 1990. The fact that Black had delayed ...Bg7 meant that he could take the sting out of White's Bg5 by breaking the pin on his king with ...Be7.

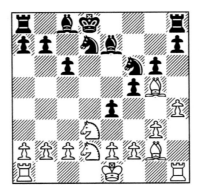

Diagram 3 (W)
Good for Black

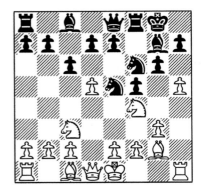

Diagram 4 (W)
Holding firm

After the alternative 4...Bg7 5 Nf4 Nc6!? White has two methods of trying to attack the black king. Firstly, after 6 h4 both 6...e5 7 dxe5 Nxe5, bringing the black knight to the defence of g6, and 6...Ng4 (uncovering an attack on d4) 7 c3 e5! create play for Black in the centre to offset the wing attack. And secondly, should White try 6 d5, then 6...Ne5 7 Nc3!? 0-0 8 h4 c6 9 h5 Qe8! **(Diagram 4)** holds firm on the kingside. Once the white attack is stymied, Black can complete his development and look for counterplay in the centre. Then White has to worry about his own king.

Finally, mention should be made of the move order 1 d4 f5 2 g3 Nf6 3 Bg2 g6 4 h4: White plays the h2-h4 move before committing his knight to h3. The line 4...Bg7 5 Nh3 Nc6 6 Nf4 transposes to the variation discussed above, but White can also play more sharply by omitting Nh3 altogether: 5 h5 Nxh5 6 e4, when Black holds things together with 6...e6!. Now 7 Rxh5 gxh5 8 Qxh5+ Kf8 9 exf5 Qe8! doesn't give White enough for the exchange. Beim suggests instead 7 e5, analysing 7...0-0 8 Bf3 Qe8 9 Bxh5 gxh5 10 Nh3 d6 etc. when in his opinion Black has the better chances.

White plays d4-d5 and Nf4: Black counters ...e7-e5

1 d4 f5 2 c4 Nf6 3 Nc3 g6 4 g3 Bg7 5 Bg2 0-0 6 Nh3 d6 7 d5 **(Diagram 5)**

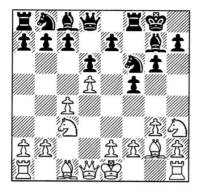

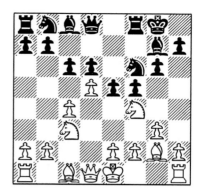

Diagram 5 (B)	Diagram 6 (W)
Preparing Nf4	Black plays ...e7-e5

White clamps down on the e6-square so that any attempt with ...e7-e5 to evict the knight when it goes to f4, or prevent it getting there in the first place, can be met by d5xe6. How Black despises the en passant rule in the Leningrad!

NOTE: Had it been invented at the time, the golden age for the Leningrad Dutch would have been in Italy before 1880, when the en passant rule was first introduced there.

7...c6 8 Nf4 e5 (Diagram 6)

Anyway! Black decides he needs to make the challenge to the white knight, as it frees his centre from the bind imposed by pawn on d5. This allows him to mobilise the bishop on c8, which otherwise would be permanently tied down by the need to prevent Ne6. It also gives his queen a useful centre square on e7.

Note that Black isn't dropping a pawn as it can be easily regained with ...Qe7 and ...Bxe6 – or at least should be! However, in the following game Black gets too ambitious.

Game 45
☐ **Y.Seirawan** ■ **J.Tisdall**
Reykjavik 1990

---

1 d4 f5 2 c4 Nf6 3 Nc3 g6 4 g3 Bg7 5 Bg2 0-0 6 Nh3 d6 7 d5 c6 8 Nf4 e5 9 dxe6 Qe7 10 0-0 g5?

Before you get too depressed about what happens to Black after this move, here is a more cheerful example after the correct 10...Bxe6: 11 Nxe6 Qxe6 12 Bf4 Qxc4 13 Qxd6 Na6 14 Rfd1 Nh5 15 Bg5 Bf6! (Black plans to neutralise White's grip on the centre by exchanging off his active bishop and then the queens) 16 Bxf6 Nxf6 17 Rac1 Qb4! 18 Qxb4 Nxb4 19 a3 Na6 and Black held the draw in Kasparov-M.Gurevich, Amsterdam 1991. Well, this variation can't be too bad if it can survive the black pieces against Gary Kasparov! Of course, it isn't very exciting for Black, which is the main reason I recommend the alternative treatment for Black with 6...Nc6 discussed in the next section.

Returning to the present game, it looks like a splendid idea to evict the white knight from f4, as 11 Nd3 h6 followed by 12...Bxe6 is unclear. But Black is in for a nasty surprise...

11 Nfd5!! cxd5 12 cxd5 (Diagram 7)

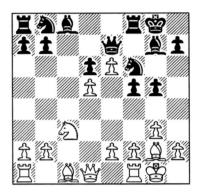 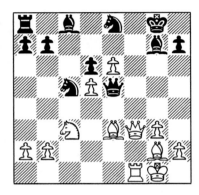

Diagram 7 (B)
Headlock on the centre

Diagram 8 (B)
Threatening Qf7+

White has two pawns for the piece and a headlock on the centre. The black bishop is deprived of the e6-square, which is his by rights in this variation. The only reasonable looking post for it is on a6 after the moves ...b7-b6 and ...Ba6: but what exactly would it attack there? Besides, the knight on b8 wants to escape from entombment on b8, and it needs the a6-square as well.

Therefore the black pieces on the queenside are in a pitiful state, falling over each other in their scramble to escape the bind. Seirawan proceeds in classic style by going for a quick attack on the other wing, as despite his piece deficit he will actually have an overwhelming localised advantage in firepower on the kingside.

12...Ne8 13 f4 gxf4 14 Bxf4 Na6 15 e4!

Generally speaking, Black is in a bad way if White achieves this breakthrough with impunity in lines after 10...Bxe6 – here it is completely crushing.

15...Nc5 16 exf5 Rxf5 17 Qg4 Qf6 18 Be3 Rxf1+ 19 Rxf1 Qe5 20 Qf3 (Diagram 8)

White is attacking with every piece, whilst the black rook and bishop on c8 are doing nothing: practically speaking, you could say that White is a rook up, even if materially speaking he is a piece down.

20...Nf6 21 Bf4 Qd4+ 22 Kh1 Nxe6

A desperate move, as White was about to demolish his centre with 23

Bxd6 and if 22...Ne8 then 23 Be5! Qxe5 24 Qf7+ Kh8 25 Qxe8+ forces mate. The rest is a massacre in slow motion.

23 dxe6 Bxe6 24 Qxb7 Re8 25 Nb5 Qxb2 26 Nc7 Qxb7 27 Bxb7 Bc8 28 Bxc8 Rxc8 29 Bxd6 Ne4 30 Bf4 Bd4 31 Kg2 a5 32 Rd1 Bb2 33 Rb1 Ba3 34 Kf3 Nf6 35 Rb7 Bb4 36 a4 Nd7 37 Ne6 Nc5 38 Rg7+ Kh8 39 Be5 Nd3 40 Bd4 1-0

A brilliant game by Seirawan.

White plays d4-d5 and Nf4: Black counters ...Nc6

1 d4 f5 2 g3 g6 3 Bg2 Nf6 4 c4 Bg7 5 Nc3 0-0 6 Nh3 Nc6

Black's ...Nc6 move seems to be the most promising response to White's delayed Nf4 approach. It makes perfect sense from a positional point of view: White has weakened his control of the centre square e5 by choosing to play Nh3 rather than Nf3, so what could be more natural than to prepare to answer d4-d5 with ...Ne5, when the black knight is sitting pretty in the centre of the board?

Note that White can't stop the ...Ne5 idea by playing an early d4-d5, so that the knight would be en prise if it went to c6 – it can jump to the e5-square just as easily via an alternative route after ...d7-d6, ...Nbd7! and ...Ne5.

Game 46
□ **K.Kachiani** ■ **E.Berg**
Porz 2000

---

1 d4 f5 2 g3 g6 3 Bg2 Nf6 4 c4 Bg7 5 Nc3 0-0 6 Nh3 Nc6 7 0-0 d6 8 d5

Whatever the merits or otherwise of allowing the black knight to go to e5, White has no intention of letting Black play 8...e5 without being armed with the en passant capture 9 dxe6.

8...Ne5 (Diagram 9)

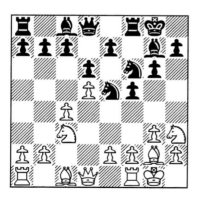

Diagram 9 (W)
Sitting pretty on e5

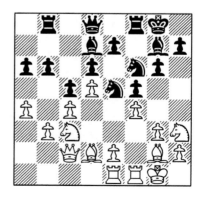

Diagram 10 (B)
Premature

The black knight can be evicted with f2-f4, but this is self-defeating, at least for the moment, as it deprives the white knight of f4. Furthermore, the pawn advance loosens the white kingside, so if it is to be played it has to be well timed. As we shall see, in this game White gets it wrong.

9 b3 c5

This is an important part of Black's plan. He fixes the pawn structure on the queenside as a prelude to an attack on the c4-pawn with moves like ...a7-a6, ...Bd7, ...Rb8 and ...b7-b5. Strategically speaking there are two good reasons for deciding to target the c4-pawn: firstly, the black knight on e5 is conveniently already attacking it; and secondly, the pawn has been abandoned by not only the white bishop which has gone to g2 rather than stay on the f1-a6 diagonal, but also by the knight which has gone to h3, whereas after Nf3 it could aid the pawn with Nd2 if necessary.

10 Qc2

A good square for the queen: she directly defends the knight on c3 against tactical tricks down the long diagonal and readies herself to protect the c4-pawn in the future. Aggressively speaking, White's own plan starts to unfold: the queen is placed where she supports the advance e2-e4.

10...a6 11 a4

White decides to make it as difficult as possible for Black to achieve the ...b7-b5 advance.

11...b6

After 11...Rb8 12 a5! b5 13 axb6 Black is deprived of the b-pawn that he wants to use as a battering ram against c4. Therefore, GM Emanuel Berg decides to play the advance in two steps to neutralise the en passant rule.

12 Bd2 Rb8 13 Rae1 Bd7 14 f4? (Diagram 10)

This is premature. White should have shown the same patience as Black displayed on the queenside with 11...b6. Instead 14 Nf4 looks best, when Black has two ways to go seriously wrong: 14...g5? 15 Ne6 Bxe6 16 dxe6 when both f5 and g5 are hanging, or 14...b5? 15 axb5 axb5 16 cxb5 and Black can't recapture on b5 as if 16...Bxb5 then 17 Ne6. Instead I recommend 14...Ne8!? on the *ChessPublishing.com* website, intending 15...Nc7, when the black knight has a dual role in bolstering the e6-square and the ...b6-b5 advance.

 WARNING: Pawns can never retreat, so every pawn move must be made with the greatest care.

14...Nf7 15 e4

We have already seen the strength of this pawn advance in Karpov-Malaniuk (Game 36). However, the former world champion had put all his pieces on good central squares before carrying it out; whereas here the white knight on h3 is sadly misplaced.

15...fxe4 16 Nxe4

Something has gone wrong with White's set-up if a knight that was performing a useful role on the queenside in deterring ...b6-b5 is obliged to recapture on e4 when there is another knight doing nothing on h3. For this reason, perhaps White should have tried 16 Nf2 aiming for 17 Nfxe4.

16...b5!

The key advance is played at precisely the right moment.

17 axb5 axb5 18 Nhg5 bxc4 19 bxc4 Nxe4 20 Nxe4 Rb2! (Diagram 11)

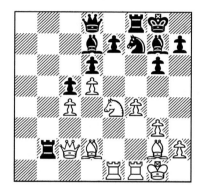

Diagram 11 (W)	**Diagram 12 (W)**
Taking over the initiative	White is dropping material

Now Black takes over the initiative. There are insufficient attacking opportunities on the kingside to compensate White for the loss of all the queenside territory.

21 Qd3 Qb6 22 Nf2 Bf5 23 Be4 Nh6!

An excellent move. The knight takes the quickest route to activity as Berg has seen that e7 is defended by tactical means: 24 Bxf5 Nxf5 25 g4? Nd4 26 Rxe7? Rxd2! 27 Qxd2 Nf3+ and wins.

24 Bc3 Bxc3 25 Qxc3 Qb4! 26 Qc1

The white queen is pushed back as 26 Qxb4 cxb4 gives Black a strong passed pawn – note that 27 Rb1 then fails to 27...Rxf2! winning two pieces for a rook.

26...Qd2

As regards pawn structure, Black will have much the better of it once the queens are exchanged, as the black pawn on e7 is much easier to defend than the white pawn on c4 – the simple ...Kf7 utilises the king for the task, whereas White's king can't offer any help to the c4-pawn. Hence, Black is eager to exchange queens.

27 Qxd2 Rxd2 28 Bxf5 Nxf5 29 g4

This leads to the rapid fragmentation of the white pawn structure, but if White does nothing then Black could go after the c4-pawn with ...Rb8 and ...Rb4 and throw in moves like ...Rc2, ...Rd4 or ...Ne3 according to circumstances. Meanwhile the e7-pawn could be defended with ...Kf8 or ...Kf7 as appropriate.

29...Nh4 30 Rxe7 Rxf4 31 Re8+ Kf7 32 Re4?! Nf3+! (Diagram 12)

Not 32...Rxe4?? 33 Nxe4+ and White wins a rook. Now it is White who drops material as if 33 Kh1 then 33...Rxe4 34 Nxe4 Rxh2 is mate.

33 Kg2 Rxe4 34 Kxf3 Rxc4 35 Ne4 Rxe4

This all smacks of a time scramble, as 35...Rxd5 is very simple. Still, the game move wins easily enough.

36 Kxe4+ Kg7 37 Ra1 Rd4+ 38 Ke3 Kf6 39 Ra7 h6 40 Rh7 Kg5 41 h4+ Kxh4 42 Rxh6+ Kg5 0-1

White Plays an Early b2-b4

This has been something of a scourge of the Leningrad at average international level. Black has lost many games to White's unsubtle plan of shoving all his queenside pawns forwards. You may recall that earlier I said 1...f5 weakened the black queenside. This was because in order to justify the pawn advance, Black has to adopt a plan that focuses on kingside action: therefore the Black queenside is going to be left undermanned and more vulnerable to attack than if Black had chosen a less committal first move. With the b2-b4 idea White intends to hit Black where there are the fewest defenders, even if structurally speaking the black position is looser on the kingside. Note that White's usual move order involves b2-b4 before going c2-c4 as he wants to get his bishop to b2 before Black has the chance to play ...e7-e5.

The reason becomes clear after the moves 1 d4 f5 2 g3 Nf6 3 Bg2 g6 4 Nf3 Bg7 5 0-0 0-0 6 b4 d6 **(Diagram 13)**.

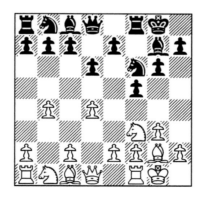

Diagram 13 (W)
White should play 7 Bb2

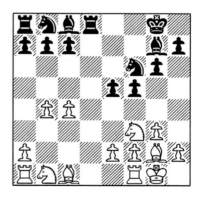

Diagram 14 (W)
The e5-pawn is immune

White can now play 7 Bb2 and safeguard the long diagonal – and in particular his rook on a1. But imagine that he played the natural 7 c4 (or that the move order had been different, say 1 d4 f5 2 c4 Nf6 3 Nf3 g6 4 g3 Bg7 5 Bg2 0-0 6 0-0 d6 7 b4). Black would have the chance to break out with 7...e5! 8 dxe5 dxe5, when the e5-pawn is immune: 9 Qxd8 Rxd8 **(Diagram 14)** 10 Nxe5?? Ng4 and White will lose a piece after 11 Nxg4 fxg4 or 11 f4 Nxe5 etc.

TIP: If your opponent is obliging enough to give you the chance for ...e7-e5 in the Leningrad then you should grab it with both hands.

Therefore 7 Bb2 is more or less mandatory. Going back a move, Black can try to exploit White's delay in playing c2-c4 with 6...d5 (assuming he hasn't played a move order with say 3...d6, as moving the d-pawn twice would be too much of a liberty). However, all the same White can build up pressure on the queenside, as the following game shows.

Game 47
□ **A.Mikhalchishin** ■ **U.Kavcic**
Ljubljana 1997

---

1 d4 f5 2 g3 Nf6 3 Bg2 g6 4 Nf3 Bg7 5 0-0 0-0 6 b4 d5

Now we have a Leningrad-Stonewall hybrid. As I've remarked countless times in this book, you have to be ready for all eventualities as regards pawn structure when you play the Dutch: it isn't enough just to be master of the standard Leningrad set-up.

7 Bb2 c6 8 Nbd2 Be6?!

In principle the development of the bishop on e6 is a useful idea in this pawn structure. It not only forces White to work harder to achieve c2-c4, but also prepares to meet it with ...d5xc4 and ...Bd5 when the light-squared bishop is very well placed. However, Black should have prepared it with 8...Kh8, when the bishop can retreat to g8 if it is ever attacked by Ng5.

9 Ng5 Bf7? (Diagram 15)

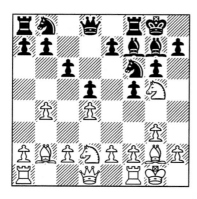

Diagram 15 (W)
Not admitting the mistake

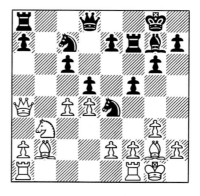

Diagram 16 (B)
Good positional play

We all hate having to admit we have made a mistake, which is normally why one mistake is quickly followed by another! Here Black should calmly play 9...Bc8 when the onus is on White to prove that the knight is doing anything useful on g5.

You may wonder why so much fuss is being made about the exchange of Black's light-squared bishop for a knight. After all, isn't this his 'bad' bishop, which is caged in by the pawns? Well, it is true that the pawn structure is blocked at the moment, but it just takes a little prodding from White for lines to become open – and then Black really misses his light-squared bishop.

10 c4

Now 10...dxc4 11 Nxf7 Rxf7 12 Nxc4 is very pleasant for White – the black bishop has been lopped off before it had the chance to go to d5 to challenge the bishop on g2.

10...Na6?

This helps White's attack along by presenting a target on a6. The lesser evil was 10...Nbd7, though 11 b5 still looks strong.

11 b5 Nc7 12 bxc6 bxc6 13 Nxf7 Rxf7 14 Qa4

Now Black has no compensation for the sickly pawn on c6.

14...Ne4 15 Nb3! (Diagram 16)

A top-class positional move. White has a simple plan to increase the pressure down the c-file with moves like Rfc1 and Na5, and so he doesn't permit things to become imbalanced in the centre after 15 Nxe4 dxe4 16 Qxc6 Rb8 etc.

TIP: If you have a big advantage, don't be in a hurry to grab material: keep control!

15...Rb8

Stopping Na5 for the time being, but now the a7-pawn is hanging.

16 Rfc1 Nd6?!

A tactical blunder, but Black was already in a very bad way as the c6-pawn was doomed.

17 cxd5 cxd5 18 Rxc7! Qxc7 19 Bxd5

White's bishop has achieved the freedom it dreams about in the Leningrad Dutch.

19...Qc2 20 Qxa7 Rxb3 21 Bxb3 Qxb2 22 Qb8+ 1-0

A methodical display by White, albeit against poor resistance. It shows the dangers that Black faces when confronted by a rapid queenside pawn advance if he isn't armed with a convincing counterplan.

So what should Black do? Before we consider this question, I want to show you two extracts from the career of the Hungarian grandmaster Lajos Portisch which point out a potential drawback to White's strategy.

White's Potential Weakness on c4

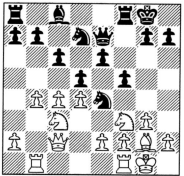

Diagram 17 (B)
An unexpected retreat

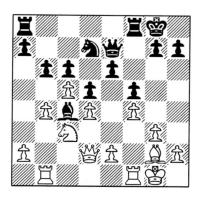

Diagram 18 (W)
A well-entrenched bishop

(Diagram 17) This position was reached in the game Portisch-Bronstein, Moscow 1959. White has just played 12 Rab1, no doubt thinking that he has a free hand to attack on the queenside with b4-b5. But the wily David Bronstein responded 12...Nd6! – an unexpected retreat of an apparently well placed piece, but there is an even better square for it on c4. After 13 c5 (not 13 cxd5 cxd5 which can only mean trouble for White down the c-file after ...Nb6, ...Bd7 and ...Rac8) 13...Nc4 14 Qc1 b6 15 Nd2 Nxd2 16 Qxd2 Ba6! (the black bishop utilises the hole on c4) 17 f4 Bc4 **(Diagram 18)** a draw was agreed, as the projected white attack on the queenside never materialised.

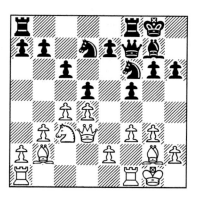

Diagram 19 (W)
c4 is sensitive

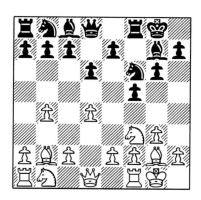

Diagram 20 (B)
Can Black do better?

(Diagram 19) The second example is from Portisch-Smyslov, Portoroz 1971. White decided to expand in the centre with 14 e4? but after 14...dxc4 15 bxc4 Nb6! the c4-pawn/square was giving him all sorts of grief. Not liking the look of 16 d5 Nfd7 when 17...Ne5 is a threat, he elected to play 16 c5, but it just made matters worse: 16...Nc4 17 Bc1 Rad8 18 Rb1 Nd7! 19 d5 (not 19 Rxb7 Nxc5) 19...b5! 20 dxc6 Nxc5 21 Qc2 a6 and White's position was collapsing.

So what have we learnt from the extracts above? Basically, that if White pushes all his queenside pawns forward he had better watch over the c4-square very closely. More specifically, we can see from the Smyslov extract that the black queen is very well stationed on f7, a base Black showed remarkable foresight in creating with 1...f5!.

So armed with some ideas for Black, we should reconsider the position after 1 d4 f5 2 g3 Nf6 3 Bg2 g6 4 Nf3 Bg7 5 0-0 0-0 6 b4 d6 7 Bb2 **(Diagram 20)** and see if we can do better.

Assuming White plays c2-c4, a logical piece and pawn deployment for Black on the kingside is as follows: ...Qe8, ...h7-h6 or ...Kh8 (both of these moves are anti-Ng5 once the black queen is on f7: in the latter case it can be answered by ...Qg8) and then ...Qf7, when the black queen is on the 'Smyslov' square where she attacks c4. On the queenside, the move ...c7-c6 is a fundamental part of Black's set-up, as it guards the d5-square and creates a barrier to the bishop on g2. It has the drawback of creating a target for a white advance with b4-b5, but Black has no choice but to accept this. Another key move on the queenside is ...Na6, attacking the pawn on b4, and this will be discussed further.

An ideal formation for White is c2-c4, Nbd2 and Qc2 and – assuming the b4-pawn has been attacked by ...Na6 – then Bc3. After these moves he would be all set for a massive pawn push on the queenside. It might seem surprising that Nbd2 is preferred to Nc3, but the point is that the white c-pawn needs a firm defence, as revealed in the examples above.

What White does *not* want is his queen on b3 and his knight on c3. This is because the c4-pawn is more vulnerable, and the queen can become a target along the b-file once the game opens up.

This is all rather schematic, so let's see how it can work out in practice.

Game 48
□ R.Bates ■ S.Conquest
British League 2001

---

1 d4 f5 2 Nf3 Nf6 3 g3 g6 4 Bg2 Bg7 5 0-0 0-0 6 b4 d6 7 Bb2 h6?!

As a matter of fact, this is an imprecision, as it gives White the chance to put his queen on c2 and his queen's knight on d2. Instead 7...c6 8 c4 Na6! **(Diagram 21)** was called for.

If now 9 Bc3? then 9...Ne4 is a highly awkward reply, as White hasn't had the chance to cover the e4-square with Nbd2 yet. Therefore White is more or less obliged to defend b4 with 9 Qb3 (here 9 a3 would be inconsistent with the plan of a queenside pawn storm). Then after 9...Nc7 10 Nc3 Kh8 (more appropriate than 10...h6, as it rules out any discovered check with c4-c5+) if White attacks on the queenside with 11 a4, Black can continue in the style of the Conquest game with 11...Qe8, while after 11 d5 e5!? 12 dxe6 Bxe6 13 b5 cxb5 14 Nxb5 Nxb5 15 Qxb5 a6! 16 Qb4 (16 Qxb7 drops a piece to 16...Rb8) 16...a5 17 Qb5 Rc8 18 Rac1 Qe8! 19 Nd2 Qxb5 20 cxb5 b6 21 a4 Nd7! Black was already on top in Van Wely-Bareev, Frankfurt 2000.

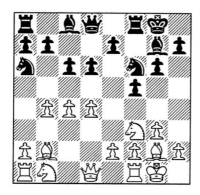

Diagram 21 (W)
The correct way

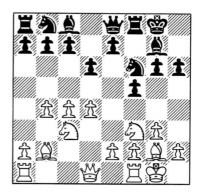

Diagram 22 (B)
Not the right square

8 c4 Qe8 9 Nc3? (Diagram 22)

Less accurate than 9 Nbd2! Qf7 10 Qc2, when Stuart Conquest would be deprived of all the tactics he now employs so skilfully against c4 and the white queen.

9...Qf7 10 Qb3

The necessity of defending c4 drags the white queen to a square where she is much less secure than on c2.

10...c6 11 Rad1 Nbd7

An important alternative was 11...Na6!?, as considered in the next note.

12 b5

Beginning a ruinous plan. He should have acted in the centre with 12 d5! when after 12...cxd5 13 cxd5 White might have a slight edge. That's why 11...Na6 would perhaps have been a better deployment so that after say 12 b5 Nc7 13 d5 cxd5 14 cxd5 Bd7 the black knight and bishop are side by side on c7 and d7 rather than both wanting the d7-square.

12...Nb6 13 bxc6?

The opening of the b-file is bad enough in itself, but this careless move also clears the way for Black to attack c4 again with ...Ba6. He had to try 13 d5, even though 13...cxd5 14 cxd5 Bd7 planning 15...Rfc8 and then ...Nc4 or 14...Nd7 intending 15...Nc5 look good for Black.

13...bxc6 14 d5 c5 15 Nb5 Bd7 16 Ba1 Rab8 17 Rb1 Ne4! (Diagram 23)

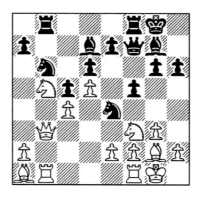

Diagram 23 (W)
Trouble down the b-file

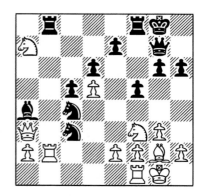

Diagram 24 (W)
Conquering c4!

All the black pieces are rapidly joining in the attack, whilst White's bishop on g2 is fast asleep.

18 Bxg7 Qxg7 19 Nxa7??

An incredibly optimistic pawn snatch, but White's position was already in danger of folding along the b-file.

19...Nc3 20 Rb2 Ba4 21 Qa3 Nxc4 0-1 (Diagram 24)

Black conquers c4 in rather impressive style!

White Plays c2-c3 and Qb3

1 d4 f5 2 g3 Nf6 3 Bg2 g6 4 c3 Bg7 (Diagram 25)

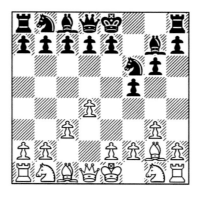

Diagram 25 (W)
White plays c2-c3

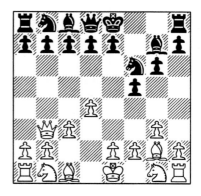

Diagram 26 (B)
5 Qb3!?

White has two main ideas in supporting the d4 pawn. The first is to play a quick e2-e4, but it misses the mark after 5 Nd2 Nc6 6 e4 fxe4 7 Nxe4 Nxe4 8 Bxe4 d5 9 Bg2 e5! 10 dxe5 Nxe5. White cannot capture on d5 without allowing Black a dangerous initiative, whether or not the queens are exchanged, for example 11 f4 (or 11 Bxd5 Qe7!?) 11...Bg4 12 Ne2 Nc6 13 Qxd5 (not 13 Bxd5? Nd4! 14 cxd4 Qxd5) 13...Qxd5 14 Bxd5 0-0-0 with an all-out attack by the black rooks looming down the centre files.

The other idea is more insidious: 5 Qb3!? **(Diagram 26)**

The idea of this move is to bully Black into setting up a Stonewall type structure with ...d7-d5 in order to secure the right to castle king-side. Whilst such a set up isn't necessarily bad for Black, it is rather rigid and inflexible, and reduces his dynamic chances. The following stunning game shows a more courageous response from Black.

Game 49
□ V.Anand ■ FRITZ/Primergy K800
Frankfurt 2000

As you would expect, computers love the cut and thrust of the Leningrad Dutch when they are playing against humans. Even if White builds up a positional advantage, a computer is so devious and concrete in its assessments that it is likely to find a tactical move to slip out of trouble, or even turn the tables with a sudden attack. The present game is rather exceptional in that the computer wins the strategical battle against one of the strongest human players of all time.

1 d4 f5 2 g3 Nf6 3 Bg2 g6 4 c3 Bg7 5 Qb3

I guess in choosing this variation Anand was hoping for a fixed centre pawn structure after 5...d5, which would curb the ability of Fritz to show off its skill in calculation.

5...Nc6 6 Nf3 d6 7 0-0?

This lets Black overrun the centre. Better was 7 Nbd2, when if 7...e5?! then 8 dxe5 dxe5 9 e4! stops the black pawns in their tracks. White would instantly regain the pawn after 9...Nxe4?! 10 Nxe4 fxe4 11 Ng5 with a clear advantage. Therefore Black would have to settle for a more modest deployment with 7...e6 8 0-0 0-0, when Black can prepare ...e6-e5 with 9...Kh8, but White can hope to keep a slight plus with 9 Ne1!? in order to get in e2-e4 first.

7...e5! (Diagram 27)

A human playing black might get worried about his king's future sitting on e8, but in fact Black's initiative in the centre forces Anand to renounce any attempt to prevent the black king from castling.

8 d5 Ne7 9 c4 0-0 10 Rd1 Ne4 11 Nc3 Nxc3 12 Qxc3 a5!

Excellent positional play from the computer. It restrains White's attempt to build up on the queenside with b2-b4.

13 Qc2 a4!

Being a computer, everything happens for a precise reason – there are no lazy, intuitive moves. By putting the pawn on a4, Black restrains White's plan of development with b2-b3 and Bb2, as 14 b3? will entail an isolated pawn after 14....axb3 15 Qxb3. Moreover, if the b-pawn vanishes White will have no way to put pressure on the black queenside.

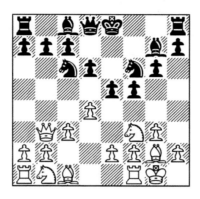

Diagram 27 (W)
Direct play from Black

Diagram 28 (W)
Preparing ...Bf5

14 Rb1

Anand therefore prepares b2-b3 and Bb2, but the computer has a tactical line ready against this.

14...f4! (Diagram 28)

Black gives up the e4-square but clears the way for ...Bf5, which would spike the white queen and rook.

15 Ng5 Nf5!

No prejudice: as 15...Bf5 can be met by 16 Ne4, Black utilises the f5-square for his knight.

16 Ne4

The white knight on g5 was hanging, so there was no time to stop an invasion on d4: 16 Nf3? e4!! 17 Qxe4? (17 Ne1 is necessary, but 17...Nd4 is horrid) 17...Nxg3! 18 hxg3 Bf5 19 Qxf4 Bxb1 is the sort of thing computers dream about in their sleep.

16...Nd4 17 Qd3 Bg4!

Now Fritz provokes a loosening move that devalues both White's bishop on g2 and his kingside structure. I find it hard to believe that all this was done with arithmetic and numbers, and that there wasn't a little man in Fritz's head saying 'put the bishop on g4, make him go f3, then retreat the bishop to d7.'

18 f3 Bd7 19 b3 (Diagram 29)

White is strategically busted. The only way he can develop his queen's bishop is by handing over the open a-file to the black rook.

19...axb3 20 axb3 Ra2 21 Bb2 Bf5 22 Bxd4

Anand seeks salvation in opposite-coloured bishops. Perhaps he was also hoping that the computer wouldn't understand the blocked position that results. However, his weaknesses on the dark squares prove fatal.

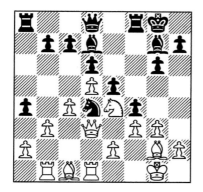

Diagram 29 (B)
Strategically busted

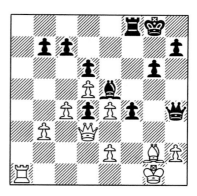

Diagram 30 (W)
Winning for Black

22...exd4 23 g4 Bxe4 24 fxe4 Qg5

Black's bishop has the powerful e5-square, while the white bishop on g2 can't be described in terms suitable for a book that might be read by children.

25 Ra1

If 25 Qf3 then 25...Rfa8 leaves White totally passive. A computer might be able to defend passively for 50 moves without any counter-play whatsoever, but a human can't live without hope.

25...Rxa1 26 Rxa1 Qxg4 27 Ra7

The beginning of White's counterattack...

27...Qh4 28 Ra1

...and the end of it.

28...Be5 (Diagram 30)

Black is now completely winning. A most impressive display by Fritz.

Here follows a commercial break: Out of curiosity, I gave this game to my own copy of Fritz 7, which I run on my rather slow home computer, to see if it came up with the same moves as played by its predecessor back in 2000. The result was startling – at least for me, having been brought up in an age when computer chess was a joke. Anyhow, up until here, my home version of Fritz suggested as best or equal best every move that Black played. And it took less than five minutes to find all the moves! Anand was far from being at his best in this game, but it is a sobering thought that Fritz is powerful enough to beat an off-form world champion using less than five minutes on its clock. A lot of world-class grandmasters have never achieved with two hours on the clock what Fritz could do in five minutes.

The result of the electronic torture was as follows:

29 h3 Qg3 30 Qxg3 fxg3 31 Rf1 Ra8 32 Rf3 Ra1+ 33 Bf1 Kg7 34 Kg2 h5 35 h4 Ra2 36 Kh3 c6 37 dxc6 bxc6 38 Kg2 c5 39 Kh3 Kh6 40 Rd3 g5 41 hxg5+ Kxg5 42 Rf3 Bf4 43 Rd3 Ra1 44 Rf3 Re1 0-1

White Avoids g3

It is actually quite rare for White to avoid the fianchetto on g2 once he has got as far as 1 d4 f5 2 Nf3 Nf6 3 c4 g6 – he usually makes his intentions clear on move two with 2 Bg5 or 2 Nc3.

White gains Space on the Queenside

1 d4 f5 2 Nf3 Nf6 3 c4 g6 4 Nc3 Bg7 5 e3 d6 6 b4 (Diagram 31)

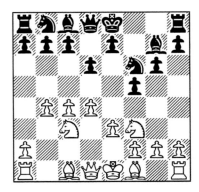 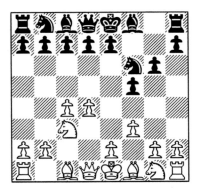

Diagram 31 (B)
White plays 6 b4

Diagram 32 (B)
White plays 4 f3

The plan of queenside expansion is much less effective without a bishop on g2 staring down the long diagonal towards a8. Black is able to reply energetically with 6...c5!. In Sulava-Malaniuk, Montecatini Terme 1995 Black seized the initiative after 7 a3 0-0 8 Bb2 Nc6 9 d5?! cxb4 10 Nb5 bxa3! 11 Bxf6 Bxf6 12 dxc6 Qa5+ 13 Nd2 Bxa1 14 cxb7 Bxb7 15 Qxa1 a2 16 Bd3 Bxg2 17 Rg1 Be4! with excellent winning chances due to the passed pawn on a2.

Alternatively, after 6 Bd3 Black can play for the advantage immediately with 6...e5!? 7 dxe5 dxe5 8 Nxe5 Ne4 9 Bxe4 Qxd1+ 10 Nxd1 fxe4 11 f4 exf3 12 Nxf3 Be6 13 Bd2 Nd7 14 Rc1 Nc5 and Black had a strong initiative for the pawn in Giffard-Legky, Cannes 1992.

White plays 1 d4 f5 2 c4 Nf6 3 Nc3 g6 4 f3!?

1 d4 f5 2 c4 Nf6 3 Nc3 g6 4 f3!? (Diagram 32)

This little pawn move may not look very dangerous, but in fact after 4...Nc6 5 e4 fxe4 6 fxe4 e5 7 dxe5! Nxe5 8 Nf3 Nxf3+ 9 Qxf3 White can build up a serious attack with moves like 10 Bg5 or 10 e5 in the offing.

Instead Black should stand his ground in the centre with 4...Bg7 5 e4 d6, when we have the Sämisch Variation of the King's Indian but with a black pawn on f5 rather than f7. One game continued 6 e5 dxe5 7 dxe5 Qxd1+ 8 Kxd1 Nfd7 9 f4 Na6 10 Be3 b6 11 Nf3 Bb7 12 Be2 Ndc5 13 a3 Ne6 14 Kc2 (surely White should play 14 b4 here to keep the black knight out of c5) 14...Nac5 15 Nd5 Kf7 with double-edged play in Lugovoi-Zhang Zhong, Moscow 2004.

White aims for a quick h4-h5

Game 50
□ **L.Zsinka** ■ **I.Almasi**
Hungary 1999

1 d4 f5 2 c4 Nf6 3 Nc3

TIP: If White bashes out 1 d4, 2 c4 and 3 Nc3 and looks like he means business, then I suggest you play 3...d6 to sidestep this sharp variation.

3...g6 4 h4 d6

A critical moment. The alternative 4...Bg7 is interesting and leads to a hard fight after 5 h5 Nxh5 6 e4!, when 6...Nf6 7 exf5 gxf5 8 Bg5 lets White build up a promising attack at the cost of only a pawn, while 6...e6 7 Rxh5 gxh5 8 Qxh5+ Kf8 9 exf5 Qe8 10 Qh4 exf5+ 11 Nge2 offers White a decent initiative for the exchange.

5 h5 Nxh5 6 Rxh5 gxh5 7 e4 Qd7!

The black queen makes an escape route for her fellow monarch.

8 Qxh5+ Kd8 9 Nf3 Qe8 (Diagram 33)

An amusing situation – the black queen and king have changed places. And a good thing it is too: the black king is well guarded by the jagged edges of the triangle of centre pawns, while the queen has the chance to become active on the light squares.

10 Qh4 fxe4 11 Ng5 h6?!

Black is understandably keen to chase away the white knight, but according to Almasi writing in *Chess Informant* he should have played the immediate 11...Bg7. Then after 12 Be3 Bf6 13 Ncxe4 h6! 14 Nxf6 hxg5 15 Qxg5 Qf7 Black has every chance to win.

12 Ngxe4

Now White's initiative continues. Generally speaking, the main drawback of having a king stuck in the centre isn't that it is in particular danger of being mated, but rather that it gets in the way of a rook in the corner being brought into action. Here, for example, Black readily develops his minor pieces over the next few moves, but getting the rook on a8 into the game proves problematical.

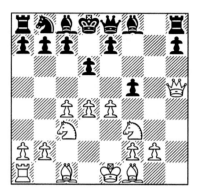

Diagram 33 (W)
Trading places

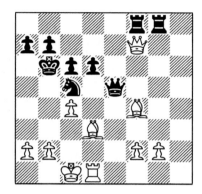

Diagram 34 (W)
The rook enters the game

12...Bg7 13 Be3 Bf5 14 0-0-0 Nd7 15 Nd5 Bxe4 16 Qxe4 c6 17 Nf4 e5 18 dxe5 Bxe5 19 Qf5 Kc8 20 Ng6 Rg8 21 Bd3 Kc7 22 Bxh6 Nc5 23 Nxe5 Qxe5 24 Qf7+ Kb6 25 Bf4?

He had to keep the tension with 25 Bf1!.

25...Raf8! (Diagram 34)

The entrance of the aforementioned rook forces White into an endgame which proves untenable.

26 Bxe5 Rxf7 27 Bg3 d5 28 cxd5 cxd5 29 Bc2 Ne4 30 Bxe4 dxe4 31 Rd6+ Kc5 32 Re6 Kd5 33 Re5+ Kd4 34 Re6 Rxg3!

An excellent decision. Black's passed pawn, closely supported by the king, will be decisive.

35 fxg3 Rf1+ 36 Kd2 Rf2+ 37 Kc1 Rf1+ 38 Kd2 Rf2+ 39 Kc1 Rxg2 40 Rd6+ Kc5 41 Re6 Kd4 42 Rd6+ Kc4 43 Re6 Kd3 44 Rd6+ Ke2 45 Rd7 e3 46 Rxb7 Kf1 47 Rf7+ Rf2 48 Rh7 Rf8 49 Re7 e2 50 Kd2 Rd8+ 51 Kc3 e1Q+ 52 Rxe1+ Kxe1 53 b4 Ke2 54 a4 Ke3 55 Kc4 Ke4 56 Kc5 Rc8+ 57 Kb5 Kd5 58 g4 Rb8+ 59 Ka5 Kc4 60 b5 Rb6 0-1

Index of Variations

Gambits, 2 Bg5 and 2 Nc3

1 d4 f5 2 Nc3
    2 g4 *13*
    2 h3 *12*
    2 Nf3 Nf6 3 Bg5 *30*
    2 Bg5
        2...g6 *28*
        2...h6 3 Bh4
            3...g5 *25*
            3...c5 *26*
    2 e4 fxe4 3 Nc3 Nf6
        4 f3 *16*
        4 Bg5
            4...Nc6 *20*
            4...e6 *17*
2...Nf6
    2...d5 3 Bf4 *35*
3 Bg5 d5 4 Bxf6 *38*
    4 e3 *40*

The Stonewall

1 d4 f5 2 g3
    2 c4 Nf6 3 Nc3 e6 4 e3 d5 5 Bd3 c6 *69*
2...Nf6 3 Bg2 e6 4 Nf3
    4 c4
        4...d5 5 Nh3 *66*
        4...Bb4+ 5 Bd2

5...Be7 *47*

5...Bxd2+ 6 Qxd2 0-0 7 Nc3 d5 *59*

4...d5

4...Be7 5 c4 0-0 6 0-0 Ne4 7 Qc2 Bf6 8 Nc3 d5

9 Ne5 *60*

9 Bf4 *62*

5 c4 c6 6 0-0 Bd6 7 b3

7 Qc2 0-0 8 b3 Ne4 *49*

7 Bf4 Bxf4 8 gxf4 *63*

7...Nbd7

7...Qe7 *57*

8 Ba3 *52*

8 Bb2 *45*

The Classical

1 d4 f5 2 g3

2 c4 Nf6 3 Nc3 e6

4 Qc2 Bb4 *111*

4 f3 *116*

4 Nf3 Be7 5 Bf4 *114*

2...Nf6 3 Bg2 e6 4 Nf3

4 c4 Bb4+ 5 Bd2 *105*

4 Nh3 Be7 5 0-0 0-0 6 c4 d6 7 Nc3

7...Qe8 *101*

7...c6 *100*

4...Be7

4...Bb4+ *104*

5 0-0 0-0 6 c4 d6 7 Nc3

7 b3 Ne4 8 Bb2 Bf6 9 Nfd2 d5 *89*

7 b4 Ne4 *96*

7...Qe8

7...a5 8 Re1 Ne4 *92*

8 Re1

8 Qc2 Qh5 *79*

8 b3 a5

9 Bb2 *83*

9 Re1 *86*

8...Qg6 9 e4

9 Qc2 Ne4 *74*

9...fxe4 10 Nxe4 Nxe4 11 Rxe4 Nc6 *76*

The Leningrad

Index of Complete Games

LaVergne, TN USA
05 February 2011
215293LV00001B/135-144/P